The Money Making Game

Organising and preparing for a
money-making event, for your
particular good cause.

Incorporating basic good business
management principles.

Ideas for special features.

Games to construct.

Prizes to make.

Trevor Davey

Dedication

- To all those that are young at heart and especially for Katie and Isabelle Lane

About the author

- The author was by profession an engineer in the transport industry and also qualified as a health and safety professional. He is now retired and working in the voluntary sector. This is his first book on a lighter subject; previous publications have been on engineering and philosophy topics. All the authors' royalties from this publication will be donated to charities chosen by the author.

Note for Librarians: A cataloguing record for this book is available from Library and Archives Canada at www.collectionscanada.ca/amicus/index-e.html

ISBN 1-4120-8679-5

Printed on paper with minimum 30% recycled fibre. Trafford's print shop runs on "green energy" from solar, wind and other environmentally-friendly power sources.

PUBLISHING™

Offices in Canada, USA, Ireland and UK

This book was published *on-demand* in cooperation with Trafford Publishing. On-demand publishing is a unique process and service of making a book available for retail sale to the public taking advantage of on-demand manufacturing and Internet marketing. On-demand publishing includes promotions, retail sales, manufacturing, order fulfilment, accounting and collecting royalties on behalf of the author.

Book sales for North America and international:
Trafford Publishing, 6E–2333 Government St.,
Victoria, BC V8T 4P4 CANADA
phone 250 383 6864 (toll-free 1 888 232 4444)
fax 250 383 6804; email to orders@trafford.com
Book sales in Europe:
Trafford Publishing (UK) Limited, 9 Park End Street, 2nd Floor
Oxford, UK OX1 1HH UNITED KINGDOM
phone 44 (0)1865 722 113 (local rate 0845 230 9601)
facsimile 44 (0)1865 722 868; info.uk@trafford.com
Order online at:
trafford.com/06-0435

10 9 8 7 6 5 4 3 2 1

CONTENTS

1. Introduction

Every organisation, that is not fully commercially or government funded, needs to find ways of funding their worthwhile activities. Throughout the year in every village, town and city there is some sort of fund raising event from the humble jumble sale to the major event attracting thousands of patrons. This books aims to provide ideas for a wide range of fund raising events. There are suggestions on the way to organise and publicise events, the features that could be incorporated including sideshows and competitions together with how to make the sideshows and games. A separate section is devoted to ideas on the production of simple and economical items as prizes for games or for sale. Therefore the aim is to make as much money as possible for the good cause and at the same time give enjoyment and entertainment to all who attend. Suggestions are made on actively using good business principles, as a way of overcoming and controlling potential problems. Never forgetting that those involved with the running of the event need to enjoy themselves and to have a worthwhile experience.

Some events are traditional features of a town or the village annual calendar of activities. Many events have been held on the same day or time of the year and people have the event marked in their "mental calendar" and changing this date could be a mistake. It is also possible that your group has established this date as yours. However, with all things it is important to keep the event fresh with novel ideas that aim for something a little different. Some changes that make the event special while retaining expected features are possible; looking at the layout of the event, the décor, advertising and the programme envisaged for the day.

People who attend the event are the most important factor in the success of the day; if they are enjoying themselves they will stay for the complete event and hopefully spend lots of money. Therefore the entry fee, cost of playing games, price of goods on the stalls and cost of refreshments need to be carefully considered; ensuring the perceived value is attractive. Importantly the cost of children's events and games should represent a lower return on the basis that most children will have come along with their parents or guardians and they will spend also. This is when a prize every time is a great attraction for children. Other incentives to keeping the event going throughout the day include announcing prizes being won at set times, people walking around with prizes being carried especially if the prize was a very large stuffed toy animal. The use of background music and lots of announcements to draw attention to the bargains available, the delicious refreshments available and the features to be experienced all contribute to the success of the event.

One problem that can cause some debate is how much to charge for games. As a guide the price needs to relate to the real cost of the prize, (or perceived value if the goods were donated) and the following table of values, is suggested:

Chance of winning	Cost or value of prizes
Prize every time	3/4 times cost
1 in 2 chances	1 1/2 times cost
1 in 3 chances	1 3/4 times cost
1 in 4 chances	2 times cost
1 in 5 chances	2 1/4 times cost
1 in 100 chances	2 1/2 times cost
1 in 1000 chances	300 times cost
1 in 5000 chances	500 times cost

There is no reason why you should not have a range of prizes with an average value, taking into consideration consolation prizes. The motive is to attract customers with some "loss leaders" that are of a higher perceived value than other prizes, to attract the players.

All similar games should be priced the same especially children's games. Stall prices should give the same perceived value for money, making sure one stall does not charge a different price for the same or similar item.

Towards the end of the event new games can be introduced to rake in those last few coins. A general auction of lots from the stalls may be a way of clearing the goods and making money.

If at the end of the event you are going to sell off goods at a reduced price, stall operators need to know the actual cost. Stall goods can be grouped together as packages or sold on a buy one get one free basis. It is better to try and recover the buying cost but if the items are perishable then any sensible price is better than a total loss. If the non-perishable goods cannot be retained for a future event they can be sold on to another organisation at cost for their event. Maximising the profit and minimising losses is the name of the game.

When planning an activity some of the suggested methods of managing the event and considering the risks may seem a little daunting, the important thing is to plan ahead. Looking at potential problems and avoiding the identified "pit falls". The ideas suggested in chapters 2,3,4 & 5 may not all be relevant to your particular event, the important thing is to think ahead. Remember large problems are only many small problems that can be tackled with reasonable ease.

2. What type of event

The type of event to be planned for depends very much on the amount of money needing to be raised, the number of willing helpers, the nature of the good cause, and the amount of money available to fund the costs of setting up the event.

There are so many alternatives for fundraising events and in some cases the money raised for the good cause may be secondary to the need to raise awareness of the organisations aims and objectives. For example, a Garden Party held by the Parish Church may help to reach out to potential churchgoers. Some schools may want to raise their profile in the community and take the opportunity to show the work of their pupils in a professional manner. In other cases the profile of the organisation needs to be raised in the public eye.

Using good business practices in planning the event helps to ensure success. One simple method is "brainstorming", to gather new and old ideas together in a democratic way. The best "brainstorms" use an independent facilitator to manage the discussion. To do this effectively the group of interested parties are asked to simply name of types of events, that can be as logical or illogical as they like at this stage, and these are written up on a flip chart. Therefore people may say things like Fete, Sports Day, Jumble Sale, Harvest Supper, Garden Party, Picnic, Antiques Valuations, Pop Concert, Classic Car/Bike Rally, Swimming Gala, Treasure Hunt, Bingo, Dinner Dance, Easter Egg Roll, Street Party, Pub Crawl, "Eisteddfod", Celebrity Sports Match, Baby Show, Quiz Competition, Cross Country Race, Half Marathon sponsored race, Tea Dance, Barn Dance, Musical Supper, Auction, Pet/Animal Show, Carnival, Sports Day (serious or fun races), Psychic Fair, Donkey Derby, Gymkhana, Dog Show, Car Boot, Table Top Sale, Horticulture Show, Disco Dance, Regatta, Sports Tournament, Car Mystery

Rally, Bring and Buy Sale. The list can be as long as you like but at this stage there is no discussion on the detail, only the basic idea. The group is then asked to vote on their top five preferences with five points for their first preference to one point to their fifth preference. The points are then added together to give a consensus of opinion on the preferred events. The next stage is to take the top five or more ideas and list the good points and the perceived problems again with just the thought but without discussion of the details. For example people might say; too complicated, no suitable amenities, lots of interest, children involvement, good for our image, not good for our image, too expensive, not fashionable, easy to organise, we have experience, we know it works.

The views are then grouped together and at this stage managed discussion takes place followed either by an agreed way forward even or a democratic vote on the event to be planned. Using this method new ideas or variations on tried and tested ideas will emerge and the interest factor naturally increases. Now that the type of event and the skeleton of the ideas have been agreed, the real work begins in earnest. Planning a year in advance is not too early especially as in the peak seasons, around public holidays; many, features, locations and hire services are booked up well in advance.

It is also important at this early stage to try and find out what is also planned by other organisations in the immediate vicinity to avoid clashes and possible lack of support.

In every event planned the first thing to consider is the available venue, is it free and if so are there any hidden costs which could be, for example, the cost of cleaning up before and after the event, the caretaker being in attendance, protection of the fabric of the building or property etc. If there is a hire fee what are the terms and conditions with your hire contract or agreement. Securing your booking may well include an up-front payment with some form of financial guarantee against the event not taking place, and possibly the full payment having to be guaranteed.

Are there any restrictions on the use of the premises you plan to use? Some organisations may object to gambling type activities that could be as simple as a tombola stall or raffle. There may be fire precaution restrictions on the use of naked flames that may affect stallholders selling candles and the like. Is there a need for an entertainment licence? How many people is the venue licensed to hold? This may reflect on the use of the venue and how the event is laid out. Consideration of the security of the premises at an early stage is advisable especially where fire exits are not on panic bolts and additional security may be necessary if the fire exits have to be kept open. The requirements for the provision of electrical and water/drainage services need to be considered depending on the event being planned. The number of toilets and disabled toilets available, baby changing facilities or how these important facilities can be provided if they are not available. Access for the disabled needs to be taken into consideration whether they are wheelchair users, visually impaired, and other forms of disability remembering the legislation that exists. It is worth remembering that some 10% of the population falls into the category of being disabled to some extent and your event may attract a high number of mobility-impaired patrons. Is there step free access such as ramps and lifts? Not forgetting access and egress for the mobility impaired that will include children in pushchairs and the older population who may have some difficulty in getting around and needing suitable seating. All public buildings in the UK are now required to comply with the relevant access legislation but this does not apply to private homes, gardens and fields. Organisers need to consider the requirements of the disabled and the mobility impaired and to ensure as far as possible that their needs are met. The facilities provided need to take into account all types of disabilities including visually impaired, hearing impediments, wheelchair users, persons using walking frames, crutches etc., and people with mental limitations; all of whom have different needs and requirements. Not forgetting facilities for guide dogs for the blind and hearing dogs for the deaf.

It is a fallacy to think that large events always make the largest profit and a lot depends on the risks and the up-front costs. The simple Jumble or Rummage Sale held in free premises has low costs and maybe only the cost of advertising and the majority income is therefore profit apart from perhaps the tea and coffee bar. Strictly an entrance fee should not be charged otherwise an Entertainment Licence could be required, depending on the licence already held by the premises owners.

The cost of organising an event can be awesome with up front investment that needs to be recouped before the profit starts to flow, only after a successful event.

The following list suggests what up front costs need to be considered and how the risks may be minimised in the event of a cancellation. Insurance cover for cancellations will have clauses that relate to the actual cause of the event being cancelled such as heavy rain resulting in an outdoor ground being flooded, or the premises being unavailable due to unforeseen circumstances that could not have been reasonably anticipated. Insurance will not cover failure of the organisers to manage the event in a professional manner. Discussions with the insurance broker will be necessary at an early stage in the planning with the premium being dependant on the risks to the insurance company. The cost of insurance may be prohibitive and perhaps the seeking of a commercial organisation that will sponsor the event, for at least the up front costs may be the best answer.

A risk assessment, with risk prioritisation, at an early stage is a good management practice; where you can identify risks and take actions to remove the risk or reduce the risk to the highly improbable. Risk assessment is a science on its own but the simple requirement is to consider what could go wrong, scoring the severity on a 1 to 5 basis. The total cost of the risk, which may be a combination of a number of factors, including your own losses, compensation to others, loss of good will, increased insurance premiums and additional work for the organisers. A failed or problem event may affect the organisations standing and the ability to have successful events in the future.

The following incorporates some of the main financial risks of the event not taking place or unexpected problems causing or contributing to a less than fully successful activity. The actual risks will depend on the type of event, number the type of patrons expected to attend together with when and where it's going to be held. The risk assessment incorporates any historical knowledge available such as previous successes and other organisations good and not so good experiences and the thoughts in hindsight of lessons to be learnt.

Note – *The requirements relating to Entertainment Licences, Gambling restrictions, licences to sell alcoholic beverages and other related authorisations would relate to local Legislation.*

Risks and Mitigation

Hire of premises. *Agreement with the hirer to reduce or waive charges in the event of your function being cancelled due to inclement weather or other causes beyond your control. Possible insurance cover or sponsorship may reduce the risk. For an outdoor event could the event be moved indoors, at the last minute, as an alternative if there is a danger of inclement weather?*

Hire of equipment. *As for premises, but consider what needs to be hired: - tents – marquees – flooring – barriers & fencing – toilets – washrooms – bunting – flags – barriers – inflatables – candy floss machines – ice cream fridges – popcorn popping machines – glasses – cutlery – china – linen – outdoor cooking / barbeques – fancy dress –*

children's amusements – tables / chairs – gas bottles for balloon inflating – donkey derby –"It's a knock-out" and other games – public address – character costumes. In some cases other organisations have equipment for loan rather than undertaking a commercial hiring agreement, so it's worth asking around. The local scout group for example may have large tents and cooking equipment available.

Power Failure. *Probably insurable provided the power failure is not due to overloading of the premises rated supply or due to equipment being used that is defective causing the circuit protection to activate. Will ice cream and other frozen/chilled food being a total lost due to failure of refrigeration plant?*

Performers Fees. *Look at contract for "get out" clauses with possible insurance cover.*

Purchase of Perishable Goods. *Consider what could be resold possibly at cost or taken back by supplier. Some items may be kept frozen for use at a later date.*

Advertising costs. *Probably a total loss and there may be a cost associated with informing of a cancellation.*

Advance ticket sales and prize programmes. *Payments need to be re-funded or re-validated for the event being organised for a later date.*

Purchased and donated goods for stalls, game prizes, raffles etc. *Is there suitable storage available where the goods will not be damaged until they can be used? Donors need to be advised that their gifts are going to be used at a later date for the same good cause. Are the goods seasonal or dated?*

Rents / site fees for outside organisations / commercial enterprises providing features at your event. *The agreements with these fee payers needs to have a clear understanding that in the event of a cancellation your organisation will not be responsible for any* *losses by these third parties and if your organisation will refund in full or part any reservation fees, paid prior to the event.*

Failure of a paid performer or feature to attend the event.
Ensure that the agreement is clear that in the event of failure to attend any pre-payment is returned in full. Performers are normally booked through an agency who may offer and alternative artiste to cover for the booked act, making sure that the replacement performer is suitable and of an equivalent or higher calibre.

Ensuring patrons will attend. *Positive advertising with the good cause clearly identified, involvement of other organisations especially where children are involved who will bring the family along to watch. Can the event be combined with another crowd drawing event such as the local flower show or dog show? Reminders that the event is taking place near the date of the event could be extra advertising, "Next Week" stickers on posters and word of mouth. Pre-purchased tickets and programmes will ensure some advanced income and hopefully attendance on the day.*

Good Will. *People still need to be thanked for their efforts including personal and corporate supporters. Possibly the most difficult risk to manage ensuring that the organisation remains committed to the good cause and will continue with their support in the future.*

With all the possible risks, it is imperative that a budget is agreed by the organisation for the presentation of an event, at an early stage of planning. Making sure that everyone is very clear that the organisations funds are at risk in the unlikely event of a failure. This is where sponsorship in full or part reduces the risk. As a rule of thumb a budget for risk funding should not exceed 20% of the estimated minimum takings on the event.

Other matters that need to be considered at an early stage of planning include: -

The legal position with regard to Legislation needs to be checked on the latest requirements that will be applicable to the location of the planned event. In addition Local Authority by-laws and the owners of the premises restrictions, this could include environmental restrictions. There may be requirements for road closures, parking restrictions, signposts, maintaining access to other properties and businesses to be taken into consideration. With all these matters suitable applications to the relevant authorities need to be made at an early stage even if it's only to seek advice on possible restrictions.

Gaming (licence) approval may only be needed if there are cash prizes - *therefore avoid cash prizes but check local Legislation.*

Performing Rights Society Licence / Music Licence – *check if the premises have a licence.*

Events in a private home/garden may only require an entertainments licence if you are charging an entrance fee – The owners insurance policy needs to be checked to ensure that they are covered for personal injury for the visitors attending. - *Check local legislation.*

Fetes and other events – *other matters that need to be considered.*

- May need an entertainment licence especially if an entrance fee is charged.
- If alcoholic drinks are being sold a special licence will be required; but this may be overcome if a holder of a licence gets the required special licence as an extension of their existing licence.
- Insurance for public liability and loss due to damage to property or cancellation if applicable is necessary and you need to know what insurance the premises have already with any restrictions.
- Music and Dancing licence may be required if the premises do not already have this licence.

- The local fire officer and police must be consulted at an early stage to ensure there are no objections from a public safety point of view.
- Approach local residents and business owners to explain what is planned and seek their co-operation.
- Prepare notices reminding patrons to be responsible for their own property and post in the entrance and other places such as changing rooms.

<u>Notes on other matters - that need to be addressed at the planning stage.</u>

4. Advertising

Advertising and marketing your event is worth spending time and energy on to improve the chances of a successful activity. The first consideration for any event is to seek a suitable, eye catching, meaningful name for the event. Think about whom you want to attract, age groups, families, employee groups, adults only and perhaps local or special interests. The name of the event needs to give a good indication of what is going to happen coupled with the clear indication of the good cause. Naming the event needs to be descriptive, eye catching, memorable and original as far as possible and no more than three or four words. A few ideas are suggested.

Not a **Jumble Sale** but perhaps, "Used & Useful", "Hidden Treasures", "Recycled but not Forgotten", "Best Bargains Around", "Bargains from Yesteryear", "Good Quality Bargains", "Quid's In", "Attic Turnout"

Not a **Flower and Vegetable Show** but perhaps, "Natures Harvest", "Blooming Wonderful", "From Seeds to Maturity", "Only Big Ones Here", "Colour and Scrumptious", "Garden Bounty"

Not a **Christmas Fair** but perhaps, "Santa's Workshop", "Seasonal Bargains", "Christmas Starts Here", "Support Santa's Helpers", "Gifts Noel", "Christmas Cracker". "Festival of Light", "Snow Time", Noel Fayre", "Winter Frost Fair"

Not a **Spring / Easter/ Summer Fair** but perhaps, "Easter Bunnies", "Spring into Action", "Daffodil Day", "Spring Bounce", "Summer Madness" "Mid-Summer Fest", "Summer Solstice",

Not a **Fete** but perhaps, "The Greatest Show in Town", "Clowns Fun & Games", "The Biggest Picnic Ever", "Celebrate with Us",

"Entertainment for Everyone", "Traditional Fete", "The Best Day Out", "Family Fun Day", "Grand Carnival" Using the word *"Fayre" instead of Fair gives a suggestion of a traditional event*

With all slogans you can exaggerate a little as long as you don't mislead people. If it's a special anniversary of an organisation then this can be used in the title of the event, such as the centenary celebrations, to indicate it's something a little special.

With the production of posters and flyers to advertise the event it is important that they are eye catching, with clear information and professionally presented. There are often assumptions made that by just stating the local name of a venue everyone will know the location therefore a fuller address and perhaps directions are desirable. The poster needs to say the obvious things such as the name of the event, the start time, date and location, what the good cause being supported is, if there is an entrance fee or if entrance is free, the main special features and perhaps car parking arrangements. If you have a web page address use it on the poster it all helps to give credibility to your good cause. The actual design of the advertising artwork need to consider the target audience and it may be prudent to have more than one design that encourages attendance by different groups and ages.

Utilising the power of today's computer programs and available inexpensive software packages can produce very professional artwork generally in A4 size, portrait mode. Using ClipArt can enhance the poster making sure that the artwork is not copyright. Posters can be produced cheaply by producing a poster at A4 size in black print and then using the services of a print shop have the poster enlarged to A3 size, preferably on coloured paper. Larger sizes can be produced but the quality of the original has to be of a high standard to reproduce well. One way of enhancing the design of the poster is to have an outline of a comic character or even a bunch of balloons that can be easily coloured in after the printing process just to catch the eye.

Another way is to add motives, characters or photographs after the printed posters have been produced to give added colour and interest to the advertisement.

Some commercial organisations like Estate Agents may be prepared to provide free advertising boards detailing the event abet with the board also advertising their own organisation.

Printed cloth or plastic banners strung across a main street between two supports or between trees at the side of a busy thoroughfare could be advantageous.

Advertising in local papers can be expensive, as you need to have a large advert to catch the reader's eye. It may be possible to get some free advertising by offering a short news item to the editor or even a letter to the editor about the forthcoming event, telling them that there are plenty of interesting things to experience. Making sure that the aims and ambitions of you organisation are clearly described and how you plan to use of the money you hope to raise. Photographs of some relevance to the story may also be welcomed. Remember local newspapers and other periodicals have publishing dates and copy in dates that need to match the time you want to make an impression. Timing is therefore of the essence, too early and potential patrons may forget, too near the event may be too late. The best option could be the free publicity one week followed by a paid for advert the next week. Many local newspapers have free "What's On" features and it may be worth offering a shortened version of you forthcoming event to the newspaper, to prevent mistakes. Look out for the other publications such as church newsletters, local residents organisation newsletters, company periodicals, club magazines, where free advertising of you event may be possible.

If you have a local radio or even television station they may well be interested in a local event and the good cause being supported for an interview in one of their local interest news spots. Make sure that whomever is selected to be interviewed by the media can speak enthusiastically and coherently of the organisation, knows the background of the good cause together with that special ability to sell the event.

Most local authorities have web pages, which detail local events and it may be possible giving sufficient notice to use this form of advertising.

If your area has a Local Authorities Information Office, telephone advice service or even notice boards, advise them and ask for a mention on their information site providing them with a suitable text.

Local Supermarkets often have a free notice board for community events and in this case they are displaying postcard size information cards. Ask the local shops, garages, businesses, sports club, colleges, schools, churches etc., to display an A4 / A5 size flyer for your event in their windows or on notice boards. When seeking agreement to display try to ask the manager or person in charge, rather than just leaving your information. If it's a recognised good cause they will be happy to oblige. Again using computer generated artwork is better than any hand written notice unless you have the services of a graphic artist to produce original displays. It's worth asking around your supporters if anyone works at the supermarket or other outlet or has a contact with one of the managers.

Flyers for your own supporters are also important, so that they are reminded and they can also hand them out to friends, family and acquaintances, to come along to support them and the event.

If you are fortunate enough to get a well-known personality to attend, make sure this is included in the publicity, to help draw the crowds along to the event.

Other ideas for advertising

5. Plans for the Day

Good planning is the secret to success, apart from making sure everyone has jobs allocated, that money floats for stalls and games are arranged and all concerned understands the arrangements for the day. With everything going on it is good practice and important to have contingency plans if anything goes wrong. Contingency plans are a risk assessment, which is a desktop discussion on how to deal with the unexpected. Some of the things that need to be considered are:

Fire risk and fire alarms – *If there is a fire risk have suitable arrangements been made to minimise the risk. This may be related to a firework display, a performance using naked flames, cooking, or even candle selling stalls. Provision of additional fire extinguishers and or the presence of a fire officer may be necessary. Some premises will have a heat / smoke detector system installed that may be activated not only due to real fire but may be as simple as someone smoking in a non-smoking environment but also by dust or high humidity setting off an alarm. In the event of an alarm activating the premises may have to be cleared till the fire brigade arrives, investigates and if the premises are considered safe, allowing people to re-enter.*

Accidents and minor injuries / illness – *Is there a need for a First Aider to be on duty? This is especially important if there are vulnerable patrons anticipated to attend such as children and the mobility impaired. Is there a need for a first aid / rest / recovery room or other accommodation?*

Slips, trips and falls – *Are all trailing cables, water pipes, ropes tethering tents, spikes, holes on the ground, slopes, scaffold supports and lose flooring adequately protected? Are there any overhead structures below 2.5 metres that need to have protection notices and warning black and yellow tape provided to minimise head banging incidents?*

Electrical – *Are all electrical supplies adequately protected? It is especially important for outdoor events where there may be a risk of rain, ensuring electrical and water services / storage are kept apart. Electrical generators used for outdoor events must be in a suitable secure enclosure to minimise risks of accidents with the actual generator and the fuel supply.*

Water – *Is the supply fit to drink, if not are there labels on the taps? If it's a country show it is probable that dogs will be brought along with their owners so remember the dog water bowls.*

Waste water and sewage – *Are there adequate disposal arrangements in place, especially for outdoor events? Are portable chemical toilets regularly checked for cleanliness and the units becoming full and overflowing?*

Rubbish collection and dispersal – *Are there adequate rubbish collection points, rubbish containers and arrangements for the removal of the rubbish from the site by a licensed contractor? Check that none of the materials being left on site, for removal are considered a hazard under environmental legislation. (If animals are present, even dogs, make sure suitable disposal bins are provided for droppings)*

Animals –*If anyone can pet/stroke or handle livestock suitable washing facilities need to be provided for personal hygiene reasons.*

Food preparation and sale of unwrapped foodstuffs – *Are the food preparations areas clean and the operatives working in a hygienic manner? Are the sales outlets clean and the operatives serving in a hygienic fashion?*

Inclement weather – *Are arrangements in place for dealing with inclement weather such as security arrangements, protection of goods, electrical isolation and suitable weather protection for patrons?*

Access and Emergency Exits – *Are all the exits kept clear whether or not they are designated fire exits and are they well signed? For outdoor events is there an adequate route for emergency services?*

Car parking – *Are there plans for removing defective vehicles, vehicles stuck in soft ground, abandoned vehicles and accidents.*

General security – *Is there suitable storage for large sums of money during and after the event? Is there any likelihood of vandalism or anti-social behaviour? To provide some form of identification for all the helpers on the day will save any possible confusion. It could be as simple as your organisations name badge. Other ideas could be used are baseball hats, sashes or a simple uniform printed with an identification motif. The identification could be linked to the theme of the event all adding to the professional presentation of your organisation.*

If in doubt on any of the identified risks ask the experts.

<u>Other identified risks and concerns</u>

6. Features

Together with the stalls and sideshows there are many possibilities for special features being incorporated into the event; some will be free and some will charge a fee. In some cases, commercial organisations will pay a fee for their feature to be present at your event if it is advertising their services and products.

The following features may be possible and will generally be free although the participants may have refreshments provided and perhaps transport and other out of pocket expenses.

Local bands, singing groups, amateur theatrical and dance displays – *They may have many engagements through the year and early booking is desirable. Many displays are linked to adult education groups or their own organisation. It may be that a theatrical group would like to promote a forthcoming show they are presenting turning up on the day in costume and perhaps doing and extract from their next production. If there is music involved there may be a performing rights fee but the group may already have this for public performances.*

Model engineering clubs, dog obedience classes, keep fit, aerobics, scout groups, model aircraft, model cars, boats and trains – *These type of organisations may well have displays that they undertake at indoor and outdoor events supporting good causes.*

Police, Fire services, Ambulance service, other Rescue services, First Aid organisations, local transport companies, military organisation – *These organisations may have display stands and vehicles which is a way of adding interest to the event, as well as promoting their own services.*

Promotional – *Some organisations may be willing to attend an event and apart from their own display give out promotional gifts and samples to the patrons. Local radio stations, local newspapers, even* *local football or other teams or gymnasiums may be worth approaching. Some of these organisations have professional entertainers and costumed characters working with them, who all add to the excitement of the day.*

Commercial stands – *For an agreed fee various commercial organisations can be invited to attend. Food, drink and ice cream vendors may be a way of providing refreshments rather than trying to organise this yourself. They are then responsible for their own hygiene, provision of materials and portable services. These commercial organisations may require electric power, lighting, water and drainage services, together with rubbish disposal arrangements. There are many retailers of all manner of items for sale and suitable at a public event; they normally have their own contacts or advertise in specialist market trader's publications. The location and size of their sales pitch will need to be clearly agreed beforehand to avoid any disputes. They will need car, van and possibly trailer parking on site or in a nearby location with access before and after the event. Take care that they understand that they cannot close their pitch and move vehicles till after the public have left at a stated time to minimise accidents and disturbances.*

Roundabouts, inflatables (Bouncy Castles), children's rides, donkey or pony rides, side shows etc. – *These can be hired normally with people to erect the equipment and may also operate the feature. These suppliers will normally have their own insurance but it is advisable to double check.*

Circus type acts – *Acts that are available include clowns, stilt walkers, jugglers, fire-eaters, performing dogs etc. Small circus can also be contracted for a total show with their own tent and seating.*

Children's entertainers - Punch & Judy – Puppet Shows – Magic Shows – Dance – Story Tellers – *Make sure it's clear what age group you aim to entertain.*

Balloon modelling – *With practice simple shapes and animals can be made from the purchased special modelling balloons or you can employ a professional.*

Musical entertainers – Could be a single performer with their own background musical accompaniment, or groups of entertainers. *These entertainers may have their own amplifiers if needed, or expect the organisation to provide an amplification system for their act.*

Disc Jockeys – May be for a disco or dance but could be employed for musical background and as the "Master of Ceremonies". *This could ensure that the public address system is used in a professional manner, forming and integral part of the event.*

Craft demonstrators – Some craft workers such as weavers, wood carvers, wood turners, jewellers, rope workers, poker art workers, glass engravers, embroiders, tapestry crafters, flower arrangers, card makers, potters, country craft persons, and lace makers may demonstrate their crafts along with having a stall to sell their wares.

Cookery demonstrators – Could be a local chef or perhaps an expert in the art of cake icing or sugar craft demonstrating their skills.

Motorcycle displays – Could be bicycles, quad bikes, go-carts, etc. *For safety reasons will need a fenced off area for the display.*

The above fee-earning entertainers can be contacted through entertainment agencies, adverts in local papers, "Yellow Pages", local clubs and organisations and web pages.

Miscellaneous

Tarot Readers / Fortune Tellers – Make sure that the readers come with recommendations and will give their readings in a professional manner. Should be limited to persons over 16 years old. Although its not needed some form of tent or enclosure with themed drapes, may be fun. *However, the reader and the sitter should have an area, which gives a level of confidentiality.*

Morris, Country, Scottish, Irish, National, Line or Maypole dancers – Maybe a suitable group is available by contacting a local club or Adult Education Class, in the area. *They will need appropriate space with a reasonable floor surface and a music system if needed.*

Face painting – *Make sure that basic hygiene rules are followed apart from using the special non-toxic face paints. Guidance book "Easy Face Painting" available as a book or electronic download http://www.easyfacepainting.com, you can also obtain kits with non-toxic paints and design ideas.*

Costume photographs – (where a selection of dressing up clothes are provided with a background board and instant type photographs are taken of patrons dressed up). Could use a digital camera linked to a computer and printer. With the resulting picture in a card frame, the profit margin could be high. Can also be done with a painted board with comic figures where the people to be photographed put their heads through a face hole. Another possibility is a costumed character posing with children or adults as appropriate.

Santa Claus Grotto – *(with a "Father Christmas" character greeting children and presenting them with a gift, however, it is advisable to have a second person in attendance in the grotto to protect "Father Christmas").* It could include a photograph in the grotto with Father Christmas.

Wizard's Castle – Similar to the Santa Claus Grotto but can be used at any time of the year with a suitable theme. It could also be "Uncle Sam's" *with presents that have an American (USA) theme,* or "Auntie's Shop", "The Toy Workshop", "Neptune's Cave" *with gifts that have a seaside theme*, "Sweet Factory" etc.

Fashion Shows – Could be provided by a local Departmental Store, Brides Wear Hire Shop, Fashion College, group of children or an Adult Education Class. A variation on this theme could be fashion from yesteryear or national costumes from around the World.

Museum of Curiosities – This would be housed in a separate tent or room and consist of loaned archive items from local companies, local transport providers, local clubs and organisations, local authorities collections, supporters and friends. Could also include archive pictures and photographs of the local area even stories of yesteryear on a display card with some illustrations. *You could charge for admission or just have it as an attraction remembering that if you have items of value, security is paramount and insurance cover may be required.*

Rocks and Gems – This could be classed as a special interest feature with a comprehensive display of crystals and a knowledgeable person to advise on the therapeutic use of various crystals. Possibly linked to the sale of the rocks and gems with associated jewellery.

Fireworks and Bonfires – Can be part of a large outdoor event but you will need to contact the local Fire Brigade for their advice and requirements.

Complementary Therapist for example - Indian Head Massage – Holistic massage – Reflexology – Aromatherapy – Nail Painting/Manicure - Beauty Treatments etc (*contact the local adult education centre, they may run courses and have students who would demonstrate their skills*).

Duck Race – If you have a river or stream running through the grounds this feature uses the watercourse. A number or plastic ducks are purchased and each "duck" has a number marked on it with waterproof marker (this could also use cheap table tennis balls or some home made boats). The numbers are sold and the "ducks" are released up stream and are caught down stream in a net. The first "duck" into the net wins a major prize. Could also be operated with a constructed waterway on a slight incline with a water supply at the highest point where the "ducks" start. With this additional construction work there could be a number or races with fewer "ducks"

Hot Air Balloon and Helicopter rides – Only really suitable for major outdoor events where a large attendance is anticipated and suitable space is available. Remember that this type of feature will be dependant on the weather.

Welly Throwing – The throwing of wellington boots at a target or the longest distance for ladies, gentlemen, young children and older children with the longest throws of the day winning prizes.

Food Feast – With perhaps Asian, Chinese, Barbeque, Beans, Country Fare, Pig Roast, Jacket Potatoes, Vegetarian, Health Foods, Cakes, Deserts / Puddings, Seafood, etc. as the feature.

Other features

7. Stalls

Stalls will vary in their type and size and they should be as attractive as possible. Perhaps the stalls can be made to look like market stalls with an awning above and the table/counter covered at the front with coloured material which for an indoor event could be coloured paper. The stalls need to be spaced out making sure that similar stalls are not adjacent to one another. It would be advantageous to have the name of the goods being offered on a banner above the stall. Suggested alternative names are given below for the types of stall.

Jewellery could be – "Hatton Garden" – "Gems galore" – "Gold & Silver" – "Pretty Things" – "Treasure Chest" – "Dingle Danglers" – "Rings and Bangles" – "My Fair Lady"

Sweets could be – "Candy Store" – "Sugar & Spice" – "Tuck Shop" – "Sticky Toffee" – "Sweet Tooth?", "The Candy Man"

Toys & Games could be – "The Toy Box" – "Childhood Dreams" – "Pastimes Old & New" – "Big Boys Toys" – "The Nursery Treasures" – "Children's Playthings"

Foodstuffs could be – "Auntie's Pantry" – "The General Store" – "The Village Grocer" – "The Galley" – "Gourmet Foods "- "Chefs Delight" –"Nearly Too Good to Eat" – "The Larder"- "The Deli" – "The Food Hall"

Flowers and Plants could be – "Blooms" – "Country Garden" – "Natures Beauty" – "Pretty Things" – "Natures Rainbow" – "Plants are You" – "Gardener's Delight"

Clothing could be – "Chic Clothes" – "Madam Pompidou Fashions" – "Styles to Suit You" – "Bargain Wardrobe" – "All Stitched Up" – "Suit you Fine"

Records, Tapes and CD's could be – "Musical Memories" – "Tunes Remembered" – "Hum Along" – "Listen Again" – "Pop to Classics" – "The Music Box"

Second Hand could be – "As Good as New" – "Second Time Around" – "Bargain Basement" – "Hidden Treasures" – "Attic Sale" - "Rummage Around" – Second Time Around"

Drinks and Refreshments could be – a typical public house sign, (not using a local establishment name) – "Pop and Sherbet"- "Thirst Today" – "The Tea Party" –"The Hungry will be Fed" – "The Big Bite" – "Hungry?" – "Tea & Cakes" – "Tea & Cookie"-"Pavement Café"- "The Soup Kitchen"

Books could be – "Reading Matters" – "Tomes & Paperbacks" – "Bibliophiles" – "Library of Life" – "Words & Knowledge" – "Great Authors" – "Bargain Reading" "Books Galore"

Other ideas for stalls

8 Games

Games are an important part of any fund raising event because they keep the patrons amused whatever their age and spend more time at the event spending more money. The games do not have to be expensive to play especially where children's games are concerned. Most games have odds against the chances of winning which determines the value of the prize being offered. Therefore, if you have a game where there is a one in six chance of winning, the winning chance should have a perceived value of three times the cost of participating.

The probability of winning can be calculated if all the chances of winning are equal of if there is a bias such as in a spinning game with some segments being larger than others. In the case of throwing dice, the chances of winning combinations presume that the dice are perfectly balanced in the same way that casino dice are totally balanced. If ordinary dice are used then there is a bias for the dice to fall heaviest side down i.e. the six face downwards (as it has most spots), with the one showing, which is on the opposite face.

Taking two dice the chances of the two dice being tossed and say the two dice showing a six, the chances of this occurring is I in 36 throws or $1/6^2$. Other combinations could be throwing two dice that give a total of seven or more to win a prize, a game of **Lucky Seven**. The number of options in the 36 combination throws that give more than 7 is shown below.

1&1	1&2	1&3	1&4	1&5	**1&6**
2&1	2&2	2&3	2&4	**2&5**	**2&6**
3&1	3&2	3&3	3&4	**3&5**	**3&6**
4&1	4&2	4&3	**4&4**	**4&5**	**4&6**
5&1	5&2	**5&3**	**5&4**	**5&5**	**5&6**
6&1	**6&2**	**6&3**	**6&4**	**6&5**	**6&6**

This gives 36 options of throw combinations with 15 throws lower than 7and 21 throws that give a total of 7 or higher. Therefore the prize should have a perceived value of twice the cost of playing but in actual cost no more than the price of playing. The chances of getting a total of seven being 1 roll of the two dice in six throws.

If you had a very large fund raising event then perhaps there could be a major prize of a car or holiday for throwing a number of dice with all dice showing sixes. As the number of dice is increased then the chances of winning becomes more difficult, with six dice the chance of six, sixes will be $1/6^6$ or 1 chance in 46,656 throws, but of course it could happen on any throw or not at all. Therefore, the prize needs to be sponsored or covered by an insurance policy. With 3 dice the chance of all numbers being the same is $1/6^3$ or 1 in 216 throws.

The manufacture of games needs to utilise scrap, second hand, free or cheap materials wherever possible. One source of the basic materials for construction, are discarded display stands from shops that with a little imagination can be converted into a game or a stall / prize display. Games need to be painted in bright eye catching colours and if possible with cartoon characters or other art work to enhance the game. Characters and logos can be pasted on the game from computer ClipArt, wallpaper, posters, coloured paper, aluminium foil, old Christmas decorations etc. The important thing is to attempt to make the game look as professional as possible and the use of lettering by stencil or computer graphics will enhance the finished product.

With all games it is a good idea to keep the instructions, the way you win and price very simple and just like bullet points, these should be displayed in a prominent position. This will save the operator from endless explanations. The ideas suggested are traditional games or perhaps new ideas to your group. Some games are available from specialist companies either to purchase or hire if it is economical to do so. It may also be possible to borrow games from other fund raising organisations.

Games to Make

Tombola – This game normally works by the use of a book of raffle ticket stubs folded and placed in a tub or revolving drum. The prizes have a raffle ticket attached to them ending in a 0 or 5 all other numbers being discarded as losers. The patrons pick a ticket from the drum and if it ends with a 0 or 5 they win the numbered prize. This is a good way of "selling" donated items that would not sell at a fair price on a stall. The perceived value of the prizes should be at least three times the cost of a go with some better prizes in the prize pool. You need to have alternative prizes of a similar value if you are offering alcohol or tobacco products as prizes if an under-age player wins.

Raffles – The traditional raffle for one or more prizes is normally drawn at the end of the event. Another way of running the raffle is to make a draw every hour of the tickets sold in the previous hour then place all the raffle ticket stubs into a draw for a large prize at the end of the event. This gives more excitement and interest to the raffle, as winners can be announced over the public address system. Sometimes the drawing of a raffle can be an overlong process if the winners are allowed to choose their prizes or it's complicated if the winners are not present. Therefore one answer is to have the names of the prizes on separate tickets so that when the raffle ticket is drawn a prize docket is also drawn, this also avoids patrons not getting what they had their eye on and any disputes. Remember to ask the purchasers of the raffle tickets to write a contact telephone number and their name on the ticket stub

Name the Doll – This can be a doll or a large stuffed animal where a person outside of the organisation, and not attending the event, is asked to give a name, which is then placed in a sealed envelope. The players write their chosen name on a list checking that the name has not been suggested before with their contact details. At the end of the event the envelope is opened and if the name is there (or the nearest suggested in alphabetical order or perhaps a shortened version like Katie for Katrina) the doll of stuffed animal is presented as the prize. A large stuffed animal is more appealing as it will suit young boys and girls and probably the older girls as well.

Treasure Island – This requires a board painted sea blue and the shape of an island marked on the board. The island shape is then filled with sand and some toy palm trees, model boats, scale figures, even a "scull & crossbones" flag or similar being planted in the sand. Wooden or plastic plant identification sticks are utilised for the players to write their name on, and then plant their stick in the sand where they think the treasure is buried. The location of the "treasure" is two measurements from a fixed point, which is held in a sealed envelope. The treasure is discovered at the end of the event and the nearest stick wins. This game can be a tabletop game or a large scale game for an outdoor event. The game can also be managed with a paper plan of an island fixed to a soft-board and flagged pins used to suggest the location.

Where do I live? – Similar to Treasure Island but using a large map and perhaps some cryptic clues to the mystery location.

Find the Station – using a large railway map is similar to Treasure Island and limits the chances of winning to the number of railway stations shown.

Guess the Weight – This can be the prize, maybe an iced cake. A list of weights in grams could produce 100 or more possible weights, the players write their name and contact details against their chosen weight. The nearest guess at the true weight, at the end of the event, wins the prize.

How many? – Similar to Guess the Weight but could be a jar of sweets, marbles, small change (for the value) or other small items.

Guess the Time – With a ladies and gentleman's wristwatch or a mantle clock the dial is covered with tape and the players chose a time from a printed sheet, with their name against times in say 5 minute slots which gives 144 chances or 720 chances if you do every minute. The winning time is revealed at the end of the day and if the dial is altered after the dials are covered then no one knows the winning time.

Pick a Straw – Normal drinking straws are cut in half lengthwise and a raffle ticket or prize ticket placed inside the straw. The players choose a straw and with a wire "key" then push the raffle ticket out to win a prize. It can be used in conjunction with a Tombola game instead of having a ticket drum.

Prize every time games

Lucky Dip – sometimes called a **Bran Tub** – this involves a number of wrapped prizes in a tub filled with sawdust, polystyrene chips or shredded paper, the players dip into a take a present. It may be sensible to have different tubs for girls, boys and adults. This is another way of using donated gifts that may not sell well on the stalls. The perceived value of the present should be the same as the cost, or higher, of having a go.

Dress of many Pockets – Someone dresses up in a dress, could be a comical dress and make-up. The dress has many pockets and a prize is put into each pocket that the player dips into and takes their gift. It has the advantage that the person in the outfit can walk around the event, approaching groups of patrons to play, who may be at the refreshment tent, rather than being located at a games stall and just waiting for players to visit. It can also be an apron with many pockets.

Ducks – Another prize every time but using plastic ducks with a number painted underneath that will relate to the displayed prize. The ducks float on water in a large bowl or perhaps a child's inflatable paddling pool. The ducks have a screw hook screwed into the head of the duck. The players have simple fishing rods that consist of a short, straight branch of a tree or bamboo cane with a hook on the end of a string.

Boats – A variation on the ducks but with the boats made from scraps of timber or purchased as cheap plastic toys.

Mystery Parcels / Hook a Bottle – Prizes are wrapped up with lose string that can be hooked out from a pile of prizes using a rod and hook. The prize can be wrapped in a box, with loose string, that makes the prize look bigger. This game is suitable for adults where the prize can be of a higher value and subsequently the price of having a go will reflect this.

It can also be used for bottles of wine and other drinks as Hook a Bottle.

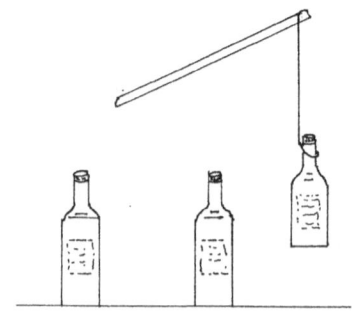

With the Hook a Bottle game the rod has a metal ring on the end of the string that is just larger than the neck of the bottle to allow the bottle to be lifted. The game needs to be organised with the bottles placed on a bed of sand to hold the bottles upright and to avoid breakages.

Strings Away –A variation on Mystery Parcels but this time the parcel is on a string and the player pulls a string to discover their prize. The game can be large or small depending on the location possibly utilising football goal posts for the frame. The mystery is that the strings are in a loose bunch, so that the player when picking a string has no indication of the prize on the end of the string.

Fishing – This is a variation on the Duck Game but is a little more complicated and more fun. The game is made from plywood with a base that supports the "fish" in the upright position as though they are poking their heads out of the water. The "fish" are hooked out using a rod and line made from a wooden stick with a string line and hook. The "fish" either have a number painted on the back or a clip holding a raffle ticket, which refers to the prize to be won. The "fish" are very easy shape to cut out from plywood, Perspex sheet or even thick coloured card with a hook at the top. The "fish" can include a "boot" or "eel" shape to give some variety. This game can be made as a foldaway game that can be stored away for use at another date.

Pick a Nail – The game is made using a hinged wooden box about 600mm square and 75mm deep. Using standard 50 mm woodworking nails, some tips of the nails are painted. If there were 100 nails, 12 should be painted red, 7 painted green, 5 painted yellow, 4 painted white, 3 painted blue and the remaining 69 left unpainted. The inside base should be about 50 mm thick and drilled to a depth of say 45mm to take the nails; so that when they are in the hole the coloured tips cannot be seen. The inside of the of the lid is used to display the winning nails, on the basis that if a coloured pointed nail is picked the value for the prize would be: red 150% of the price per pick, green 200%, yellow 250%, white 300% and blue 350%. An unpainted nail winning nothing in this game. This gives a profit, with this example, if all the nails are picked, of 46.5%. The nails can of course be replaced away from the view of the potential players as the event progresses. The game is transported with the nails in place and the lid closed with a catch. The game could also be made with de-headed matchsticks (craft matchsticks could be used) or toothpicks in place of nails.

Golden Eggs – The game is a simple picking game where the player chooses a "golden egg". Underneath the eggshell there is hidden either a coin of higher value than the cost of the game or a token for a consolation prize. The eggshells must be washed to remove any unwanted smells. For the best effect the eggshells should be sprayed with a gold lacquer or paint.

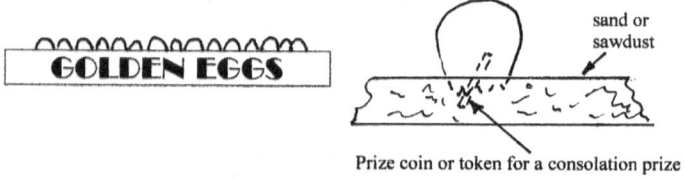

Prize coin or token for a consolation prize

Roll a Ball – The game can be constructed as a large outdoor game or small game for indoor use. The player has four balls, which are rolled down into either numbered slots or openings. When all four balls have been played the total score is counted. If you have ten slots numbered 1 to 10 then you can score over 30 to win a prize. The slots should only take one ball and the side slots are low numbers (this prevents the players rolling balls down the side bars to get into the high score slots). Because this is a game of skill rather than chance only by getting a high-numbered slot is a win possible. Variations on this game is possible, by having a board with ten holes drilled slightly smaller than the diameter of the ball, which for a smaller game could be large glass marbles. The holes are positioned in a pattern of three rows and you could have 20 holes to ensure a quicker game, with only 10 holes the operator will have to return balls that have not found a hole, for the player to try again. To make the game more difficult you can place the board on a slight slope with pegs that cause obstacles or humps on the boards surface to deflect the rolling balls and make it more a game of chance. To make the game easier you can have the holes with six different colours around 20 holes and the player has to get either all four balls in the same colour or one ball in four different colours.

Another version is as a tabletop game where the players roll six balls, golf balls, billiard balls or similar down the board and into seven possible slots. The slots are numbered as follows: 2 end slots valued at 1 point, 2 slots valued at 2 points, 2 slots valued at 3 points and the centre slot valued at 4 points. With all six balls in the slots the total value has to add up to 7 or 10 or 15 or 18 or 21 or 24 to win a prize. This gives a 50/50 chance of winning but the game can be made harder by having a winning score, lower than 12 or higher than 21.

Sam at the Dentist – This is a throwing game where the idea is to knock out the teeth in "Sam's" mouth with balls. The construction is simply a sheet of timber with a face painted on the board with the mouth wide open. The teeth are wooden pegs, which are placed behind the board preferably on hinges so that when a ball hits the "tooth" it falls back out of sight. The face board is fixed to a table with a white sheet fixed below the neck making the body shape. The number of teeth knocked out wins the prize, which could be a toothbrush or novelty joke dentures. A simple crank can be incorporated to reposition the teeth after they have been knocked back.

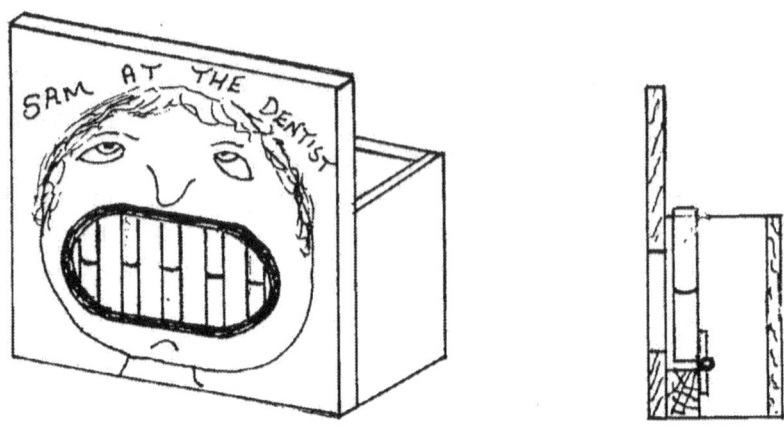

A Pill for the Clown – Similar to Sam at the Dentist but this time using white balls, (the "pills") thrown at the painted face and into the mouth where they drop into a box at the base of the board for a prize. The prize can relate to the number of pills that go into the mouth. The face is shown as a clown as this is an easy picture for the non-artistic to draw but any face can be depicted and the name of the game altered to suit.

Electric Eel – A game that requires a steady hand with the ring being moved from one end of the "eel" to the other without the ring touching the "eel". If the ring touches the "eel" a bell rings and or light is illuminated. The "eel" is made from copper rod and the ring is metal. The electrical supply should be a battery, no more than 4.5 volts.

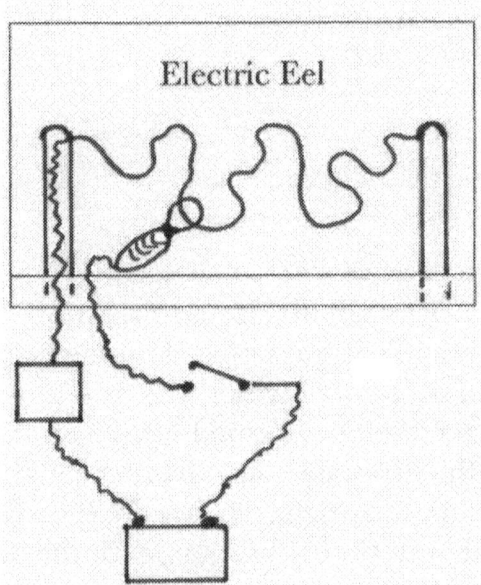

Battery with isolating switch and buzzer/lamp

Spat the Rat – The object is to spat the rat as the "rat" which is a cloth bag filled with sand, as is comes out of the bottom of the drain pipe. A standard stepladder allows the operator to reach the top of the drainpipe in safety. A game that is not as easy as it looks with a prize if you hit the "rat".

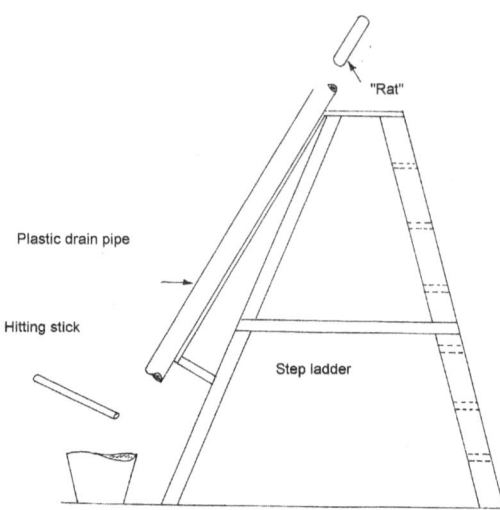

Diving Pennies - Using a tank of water a number of high value coins or coins in small cups are placed on the bottom. The idea is to drop coins into the tank of water (the coin must not be held under the water before it is dropped otherwise the game will be too easy), and if the dropped coin covers the higher value coin or goes into the cup, the prize coin is won. It can be used with a fish tank or a bath, but probably a game for the outside, as there will be pools of water on the floor.

Treasure Chest - A wooden chest is made with a lid that is secured with a pad-lock. The pad-lock has a number of similar keys, (at least six keys are needed), and the player chooses one key to attempt to open the treasure chest. If they pick the right key they win the treasure in the chest. Can also be done by having a small door in a display board with a lock to open the door where the prize is behind the door.

Cats on a Hot Tin Roof – This game can be good fun as it consists of throwing "fish" at a number of cats sitting on a wall at night and making a cats chorus (with a tape recording of cats or perhaps the famous operatic chorus). The game is made as shown below. The objects to be thrown at the "cats" to knock

them down and win a prize are fish shaped missiles made as
stuffed toys filled with beans.

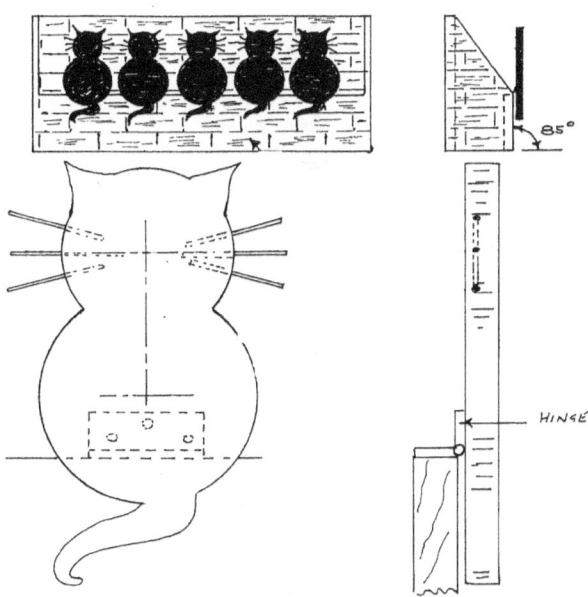

*The cat shape is cut from timber sheet and the whiskers are made
from wire, the shape is painted either black or another suitable
colour to represent the cats fur. The shape depicts the back of the
cat. The "cats" are on hinges so that they drop down when hit.*

Skittles – The game of skittles requires a reasonably flat
surface for players to bowl a hard ball, from a starting line
to try and knock the skittles over. The skittles can be the
traditional ninepins or just a number of objects that have to
be knocked over. The skittles could be a block of wood with
a picture of a cartoon character, old chair legs or perhaps a
short length of plastic drainpipe half filled with concrete.
The skittles can be hinged on a board so that they can be re-
set in the vertical position with a string hung over a pole
above the skittles.

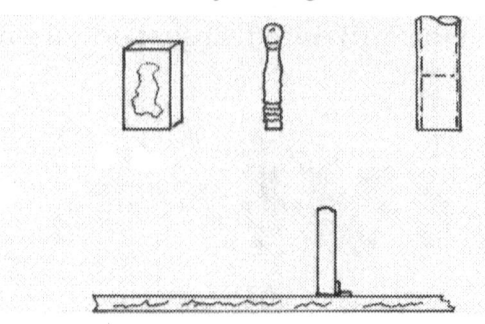

Humpty Dumpty - Similar to the Cat Game but a single shape of "Humpty Dumpty" sitting on a wall, with soft balls thrown to try and knock him off the wall. An alternative is to make the egg shaped "Humpty Dumpty" in sections so that if the head is hit the egg breaks and the pieces fall down.

Spinners – The basic idea with all spinners is where a number of players purchase a chance to win and only one of the player wins. There can be any number of winning chances but a maximum of 10 chances is suggested because you have to get all ten chances sold before the game can be played, so if the event is small then a lower number of chances may be more appropriate. The spinner has to be balanced, not to the same extent as a "Roulette" wheel but it must not be biased to stopping in the same place. If the spinner is going to be horizontal one easy way is to obtain a device used for turning a cake when it is iced, called a "Lazy Susan". This provides a base for the disc marked with the segments.

A variation of the horizontal spinner is to utilise a toy clockwork train set with a circular track, with prize stations around the track. The train stopping at the prize station, when the clockwork spring runs out.

If you consider a vertical spinner the use of an old bicycle wheel mounted in front forks will provide a balanced spinner base. The front side of the wheel is covered with a circular piece of card marked out with the spinner segments. It would also be advantageous to fit a piece of rubber to engage in the wheel spokes at the rear to slow the spinner down and hold it in position at the stopping point.

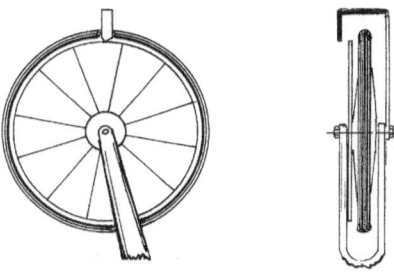

To avoid problems with the spinner being balanced the spinner disk can be driven from an electric motor either geared to a slow speed or if it is a DC motor by the use of a variable resistance. The electrical supply is on a timer switch, set for say one minute; this will stop the spinner at random without the operator being involved

Film or Television Stars – This is similar to a spinner but uses an electrical motorised switch that turns on one lamp at a time against the name of a personality. The electrical supply has a timer switch that stops the game with just the winning light illuminated. Can be made as a tabletop game or as a large feature with bells or buzzers also ringing when each light is on.

Trumps – Is another version of the spinner either motorised or hand operated, with the disc divided into four quadrants, one for hearts, clubs, spades and diamonds. The use of a standard pack of playing cards can be used for players to pick a card that refers to their winning chance on the spinner.

Golf Tournament – Using a course with obstacles with hoops or gates to pass the ball through. The player completing the course within a set number of strokes to reach a target wins a prize. Could also be the hitting of six balls towards a target board that has a number of holes that the balls have to enter to win a prize.

Open the Door –This is an automatic spinner for one player at a time. The spinner is operated on a geared motor revolving at 10 revolutions per minute. When the ball is rolled down a path to hit the hinged door (staying in a indentation to hold the door open) and operates a micro switch. The micro switch is wired to the normally closed contacts so that when the switch opens by the action of the door, it turns the motor supply off. The spinner pointer stops at a segment on the disc to win a prize. The game is made in a wooden case that is locked to secure the electrical components.

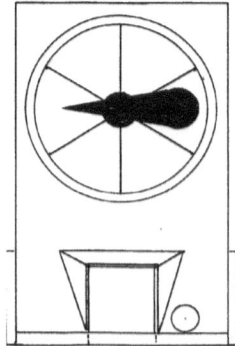 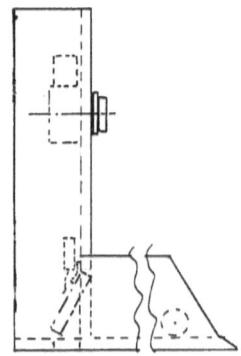

Darts – This involves throwing darts at a target. The target could be playing cards where spiking the heart, diamond, clubs or spades sign on the card wins. Another way is to have small sealed envelopes with a coin inside, the dart has to spike the envelope and stay in, if it hits the coin in the envelope, it will not stay and the player losses. You can hang a number of balloons from an overhead structure and throw the darts to burst the balloon; it can be funnier if some of the balloons are filled with confetti or even water that will go everywhere when the balloon bursts.

Balloon Race – Traditionally this game involved a card being attached to a balloon with a prize for the card returned from the farthest distance. Today this may be more difficult because of the cost of postage and causing litter to be strewn across the countryside. Another way is to have a track with various obstacles requiring the player has to guide a balloon down to a target at the end. The balloon is either knocked with the hand or by a simple bat like a plastic fly swat down the track. The prize is won if the player gets the balloon through all the obstacles and into a container at the end, without bursting the balloon or loosing it.

Mad Hatters – An alternative to the Coconut Shy, where poles are driven into the ground or supported on a base and hats are placed on the pole tops. The idea is to throw balls at the hats and knock them off. It could also be an **Aunt Sally** game if instead of poles the shape of a human body was manufactured and the hat placed in position again to be knocked off or Aunt Sally knocked over. The back can be a wall or a cloth with side sheets to retain the balls. The hats will need to be partly filled with paper to make sure they stay firm and can fall off the pole without too much difficulty.

Juggling Clown – This game is a spinner with a difference in that it only needs one player at a time and gives a prize every time. A simple case is made with a spinning disc inside that is drilled with a number of holes at an appropriate diameter and the holes take coloured lens or coloured plastic or glass on the back surface of the disc. These coloured holes become the "juggling balls". An electric lamp is positioned at the top centre of the revolving disc so that the light shines through the "ball" as the revolving disc stops at a coloured "ball" at the top, which represents the prize to be won. As the disk protrudes at the top of the case, this allows the operator to spin the "juggling balls" disk by hand. The prizes are displayed in trays at the bottom of the case. The case size will depend on if the game is going to be used indoors or outside but needs to be at least 600mm high and 400mm wide. The lamp could be battery powered with a mirror behind the lamp to magnify the light beam. A good game for younger children to be attracted to and the clown could be changed for a teddy bear or other character with prizes linked to the character depicted.

 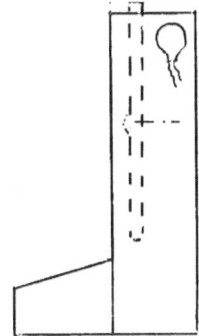

Hoopla – the Showman's version is based on a prize that is placed on the top of a wooden box, which only just allows the hoopla ring to pass over the square base; the ring having to land flat to win the prize. This makes the game look easy but it is very difficult to win. For a less difficult game the hoopla rings can be thrown onto vertical pegs on a base or hooks on a vertical board. If circular rings cannot be purchased or manufactured as discs; a simple alternative is a square ring using plastic electrical circular conduit with 90-degree bends all glued together to make a "square ring". Another way is by the purchase of rubber sealing rings or discs cut from sheet timber, rubber, plastic or thick card.

The pegs or hooks can be numbered, labelled or colour-coded to indicate the prize for getting the hoop over the peg.

Jam Jars - Similar to a hoopla but uses empty glass jam jars or bowls (or other containers) with a prize placed inside the container. The players try to throw table tennis balls into the containers and if they succeed they win the prize inside.

Ring my Bell

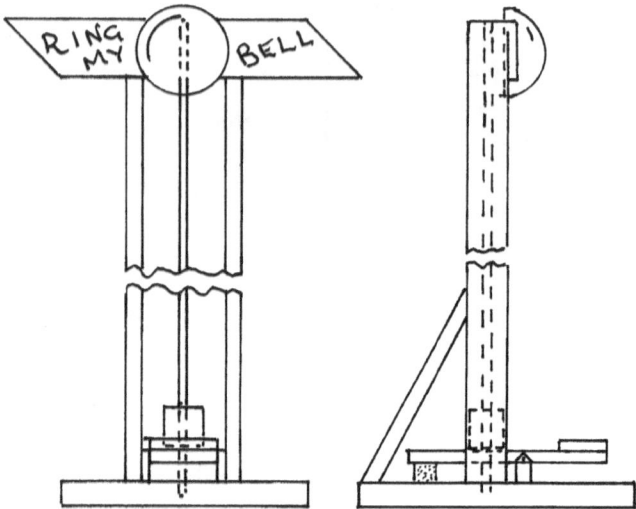

This game can be constructed either for children or adults and made to a size to suit the event. The construction is a solid base that has a pivoted lever that is hit with a rubber mallet or wooden hammer. The hitting of the lever sends the "dolly" up a vertical metal rod that is supported by a frame. If the "dolly" reaches the top it rings the bell. Ringing the bell sends out a message that someone has been successful and received a prize.

Jumping Jacks - This game is constructed in a cabinet with a glass front and air vents at the top with an inner cowling. An electric fan is fitted at the bottom that when turned on blows coloured table tennis balls around that eventually go into one of the coloured cups at the back to win a prize if the colour of the ball going in the cup matches that colour. To release the balls the cups have a handle at the back of the cabinet that turns the cups over to release the balls for the next game.

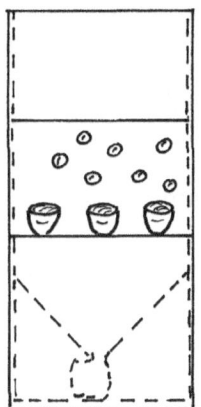 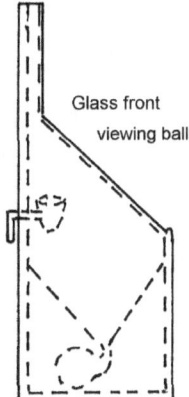

Glass front
viewing balls

Prize Cards - A pack of standard playing cards are laid out on a table with a prize against each card. The players are asked to choose a card from a second pack of cards face down and their prize is the card they have picked from the pack.

Royal Family - A pack of cards, including the Jokers are laid down randomly on a tray and the player picks a card. If the card is a King, Queen or Jack they win a prize, if it's a Joker they win a booby prize.

High Roller - The player takes six cards from a deck of shuffled cards, if the card values add up to more than 50 based on Jack = 11, Queen = 12, King =13, Ace = 1 (other cards at face value) s/he wins a prize. It can be made more difficult by increasing the winning score up to the maximum of 76 (4 Kings +2 Queens). Needs a display board with the card values clearly identified.

Tin Can Alley – The game consists of stacks of six empty cans placed on a flat shelf. The players are provided with soft balls and are asked to knock the pile cans off the shelf to win a prize. The cans are simply provided by saving a number of tin cans, removing the labels then painting in bright colours.

Sweet Shop – Similar to the Tin Can Alley but boxes of sweets being used and if the box is knocked off and the box of sweets is given to the player as the prize. To make the game harder make woollen "pom-poms" these are soft and more difficult to throw. *See section on prizes to make pom-poms. Alternatively small squares of sponge rubber could be used as the throwing missiles.*

Ball in the Bucket - Using a number of plastic buckets fitted onto a wooden board with the buckets tilted slightly, the players try to kick "footballs" into a bucket. If the ball stays in the bucket a prize is won, that could be a football.

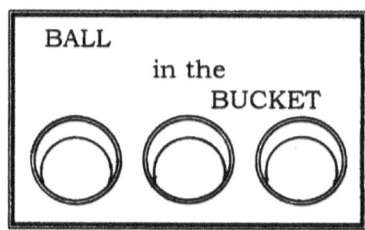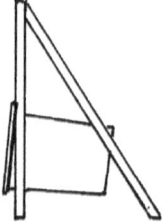

Human Fruit Machine - The human fruit machine requires a "barker" to take the money and give out the prizes with three people who are the human fruit machine. They each have a box or identical objects which should be pieces of fruit and a block with "bar" painted on. When the game starts the three people move their arms in front of them in a rolling motion reciting the following jingle:-

1 2 3 here we go
When we stop nobody knows
Will you win or will you fail
Wins for you, you never know
Are we slowing – here we go
Picking the winners
1 2 3 here we go
(Then - to suit the result)
an apple
an orange

The Money Making Game

a banana
go on have another go
        or (3 the same)
        a bar
        a bar
        a bar
We have a winner
Go on have another go

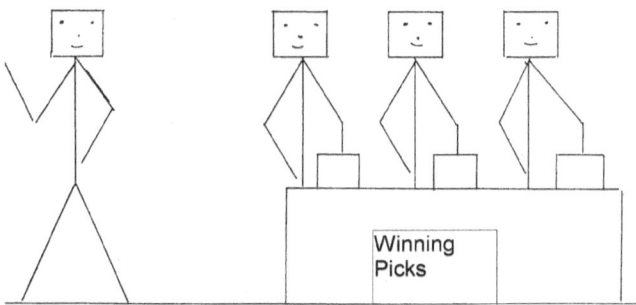

Mouse Holes - This is a simple electric table game where the idea is to find which hole the mouse is behind. The players have to roll one ball into one of five holes and if the ball gets into the right hole a buzzer or light goes off and a prize is won. After each game the switches are altered to give a new winning hole. The simple circuit is shown below.

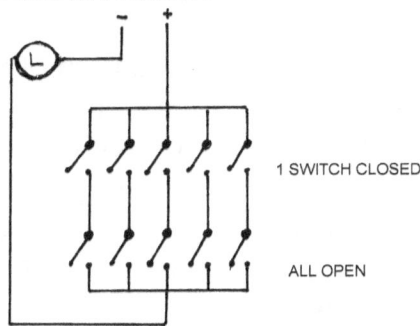

The load "L" can be a light box that consists of a picture of a mouse or even a toy mouse that is within a box with a glass front, painted matt black inside. When an electric lamp goes on the "mouse" is illuminated. The other method is to have a "mouse" fitted to a counter-balanced arm that is located behind the game backing board; the arm being released by an electric magnetic coil, with an additional switch that turns the current to the coil off once the arm is released. The cross-section of the game shows the arrangement of the switches and the return path of the balls.

Coin Path - The idea is to place small value coins on a pathway and every so often there is a mystery envelope. The players place their coins on the path and when they reach a point on the pathway that corresponds with a mystery envelope they open the envelope. The envelope could give a prize or contain a joke or a consolation prize.

This game requires a table that has a path of tape fixed to the surface with the mystery envelopes, say every ten coins, so that the players will place more than one coin on the pathway. If used as an outdoor event the coin path could be on a solid pathway using self-adhesive plastic tape. The game could also be linked to prizes that have a garden theme and then called **"Down the Garden Path"**.

Roll a "Penny" - A board is made with a lip around three sides (to stop the coins rolling off). The board is marked with squares

The Money Making Game

or circles that indicate a win value. The coin is rolled down a shoot and if it stops inside the square or circle the value shown is paid out. The "penny" may need to be a higher value to make the game worthwhile unless it's a fun game.

The coin shoot can be made from plastic sheet, thin timber or card. The coin shoot will need to suit the chosen value of the coins being used and allow the coin to roll freely down the shoot. The base needs to be 150 mm long with the steady at the rear being about 50 mm wide.

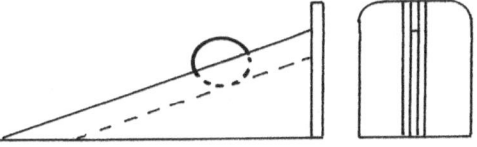

Coconut Shy – A traditional fun-fair game that may be hired. Otherwise the game can be manufactured with metal rods that have a loop at right angles at the top to rest the coconut on, with the rod driven into the ground. An alternatively it could be wooden stakes that support the coconuts in a hollow shape at the top. The coconuts are, possibly knocked off their stands, by the players throwing wooden or hard balls in the direction of the coconuts. Make sure that there is a substantial backcloth to containing the balls that miss the coconuts.

Penny for the Guy - This game requires the players to toss coins at the moneybag, with the money in the bag forming the jackpot prize. When there are sufficient coins to drop the bag down the character moves its arms and lifts its hat, and the person throwing the last coin wins the jackpot. A counterbalance at the rear of the character controls the weight of coins, required to lift the hat. All the coins that miss the moneybag are the profit, so a game that cannot be a looser for the organisation.

55

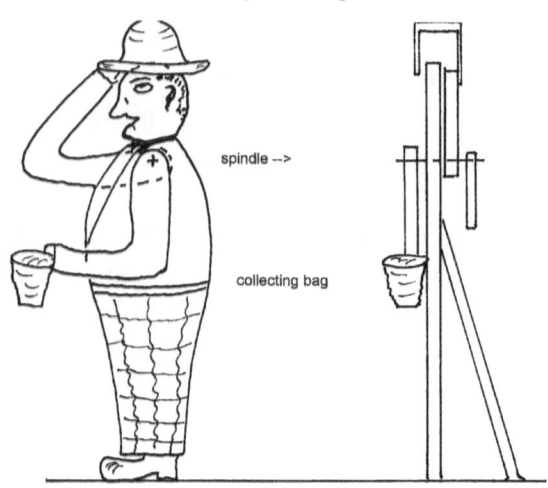

spindle -->

collecting bag

The character, which should be life size, is made from sheet timber and supported at the back by a stay. The right arm holds the moneybag or box. The left arm is connected to the hat, which sits over the head of the character. The arms are on a central spindle with a counterbalance on the same spindle. The spindle should be supported on a metal plate or bearings either side of the torso of the character and move with ease. The counterbalance can be a movable weight on a rod to allow adjustment of the size of the jackpot.

Have a Smashing Time - The idea is to smash old items of crockery by throwing hard balls at the crockery placed on tables, shelves or suspended from strings. This requires an enclosure on three sides, which could be old curtains and a cloth base so that the broken crocks can be collected safely and placed into a suitable container. There are no prizes just the fun of smashing the crockery. The crockery is old, damaged items that are just rubbish and of no value.

You can incorporate breakable containers filled with coloured liquid, feathers or confetti that will make a real mess when the container is smashed. It would also be possible to use bottles filled with fizzy liquid that will burst with a good shower adding to the excitement. Old electric lamps can be used but do not use fluorescent tubes due to the hazard of the interior coating (these tubes have to be disposed of by a licensed contractor).

Have A Smashing Time – How Many Can You Smash?

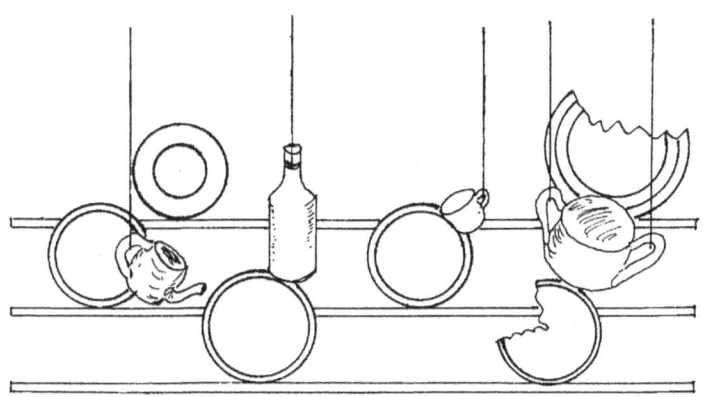

Pelt the Varlet - The nature of this game is to throw wet sponges at one of the helpers who is either held in a mock-up of an old fashioned stocks or perhaps tied to a chair. *(A varlet is an old English name for a serving wench or maid but another charter in costume could be used and the name of the game modified to suit)*

Flip a Coin - A number of flippers are made and clamped or screwed to a base that is at table height. The coins have to be flipped into receptacles or onto markers to win prizes. The game can also use small balls or even small stuffed animals such as a frog shape, then modifying the name of the game to suit such as

Jumping Frogs - The flipper can be made of wood or metal and sized to suit the coins that are to be flipped. The flipper can be made, small enough, to be pressed by finger pressure or made larger so that the flipper can be hit with a rubber mallet especially if you are going to have "Jumping Frogs.

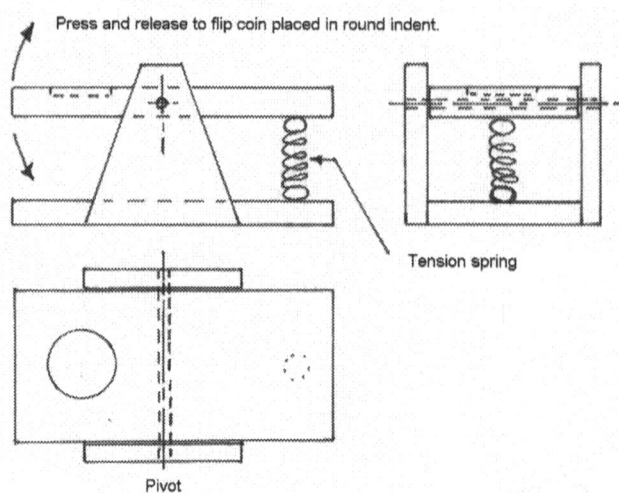

Press and release to flip coin placed in round indent.

Tension spring

Pivot

The Amazing Maze - The object of the game is to trace with a pencil a path of a maze on a paper map. The player is looking at a reverse image through a mirror and wins a prize if they can get from the start to the finish without going off the path.

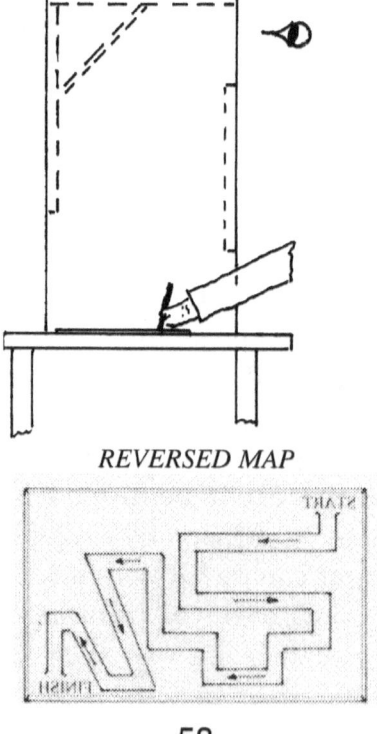

REVERSED MAP

The game is constructed as a wooden box with a viewing slot at the top where the player looks into a mirror angled at 45%. The player puts their hand through a slot at the bottom covered with a curtain and attempts to trace the correct path on the map. The box needs to be open at the back below the mirror or fitted with an electric light, to allow the map to be seen. The game stands on a table and can be used for all sorts of events that are indoors and out. The map size is preferably, A3 size photocopy (which can be from an original A4 document), with the start and finish printed in reflection.

The Money Tree - The players throw soft balls at the "tree" to try and get a ball into the bag at the end of the tree branches. If they succeed they have the coins that have been put in the bag or a small prize. The bags will have different amounts of money but at least a little more than the cost of playing. The game needs a backcloth or to be played against a wall.

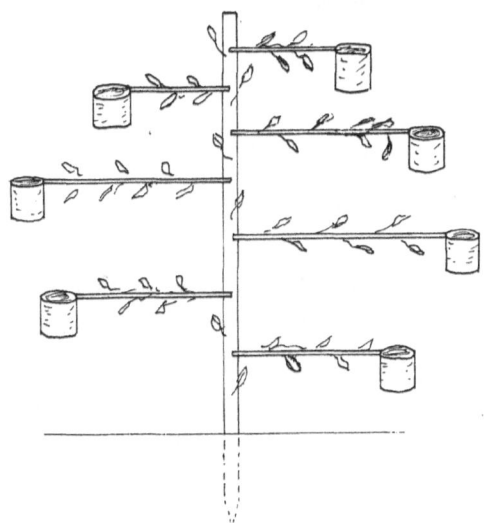

The game is made with a heavy-duty broom handle, bamboo stalk or similar, being about 2 meters long for the trunk of the tree. The branches are made from canes that are glued into holes in the "tree truck". The bags are cloth bags with a wire in a circular shape sown into the open end, and then fitted into the ends of the canes. To be more realistic the bags could be bank cash bags with the name of the bank/s printed on the outside.

At the Races - A large game representing a horse race that is more suited for the bigger outdoor events or a large hall. The game needs six players to participate each player riding a "horse" down the dedicated track. The game gives the opportunity for plenty of audience participation, in calling for the winning horse and the rider.

The players should be dressed in jockey's colours that could be a coloured sash, large coloured cap, waistcoat or a large rosette to identify the runners. The horses can be as shown below or as large cardboard or sheet timber horse shapes that are painted and fitted with straps for the participants to wear.

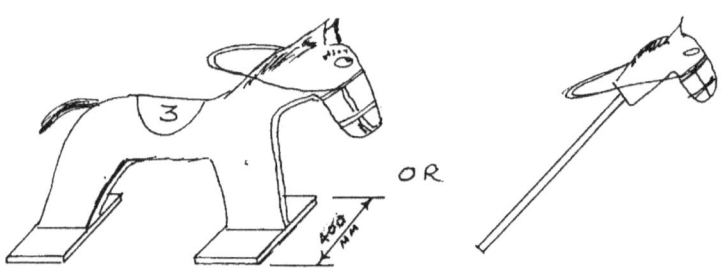

The six horses have to be the same pattern with different names and colours. The track is marked out with six lanes divided into fifteen segments. Either a spinner marked 1 to 6, or large dice is used to move the players on one segment at a time if their track number comes up on the spinner or dice. The first over the line is the winner. The prize could be a trophy with each race called a different name and run a defined times, just like a real race meeting.

The game can also be made a tabletop game using models of racing horses.

It is also possible to link the races with a "tote" system for others to bet on the winning horse. Or you could sell owners and riders tickets with prizes for both parties; this would encourage parents to be owners if the child was the jockey.

Car race - A variation of the Horse Race is a car race where this time you have a racetrack either with mock-up of six cars with players sitting in the "car" or as a tabletop game with six model racing cars, and a suitable back board depicting a racetrack with six numbered lanes. You will also need a spinner with 12 segments with the following instructions that need to be called out by the operator with a suitable patter to match the game.

- Pit stop for cars 2&3 others one move
- All cars stop due to rain
- Pit stop for cars 4&6 others one move
- Bend slow down, all cars miss a go
- All cars one move
- Pit stop for cars 1&5 others one move
- Car 3-3moves, car 5-2 moves, car 2-1 move
- Car 5-3moves, car 2-2 moves, car 3-1 move
- Car 2-3moves, car 6-2 moves, car 5-1 move
- Car 4-3moves, car 2-2 moves, car 4-1 move
- Car 1-3moves, car 3-2 moves, car 6-1 move
- Car 6-3moves, car 4-2 moves, car 1-1 move

Wishing Well - This game is a mock up of a traditional wishing well where patrons toss coins into the well to a make a wish. At the bottom of the well there are one or more containers, with a striking plate linked to a micro switch that operates if a coin lands in the container. A buzzer or bell rings and the person who tossed the coin in has a prize linked to a wish. The striking plate needs to be hinged with a method of removing the coin from the striking plate and re-setting the game. The switch operation could set off a tape recorder with a loop tape that perhaps has a recording of the "Jack and Jill" nursery rhyme or perhaps the song "Three coins in the fountain", to add an additional interest feature to the game.

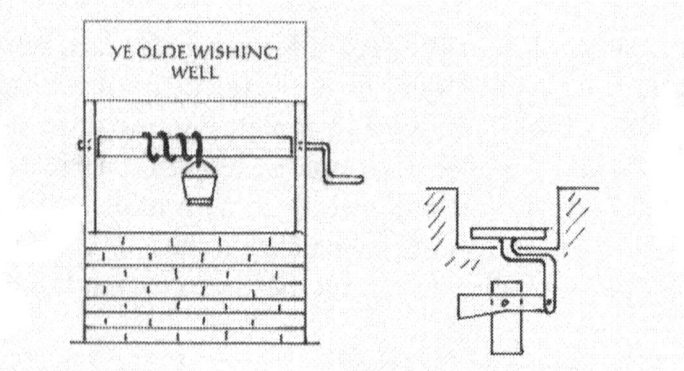

Detail of coin activated micro switch

Stepping Stones - This game is made using pressure pad switches that close the circuit when the pad is trodden on. The game requires 14 pressure pads with the first row having two pad switches on and three pad switches off, second row having two pad switches on and two pad switches off, third row two pad switches on and one switch off with the final row having one pad switch on and one off. The circuit includes a loud buzzer so that if a player steps on a "stepping stone" that is on, the buzzer goes off, and the player leaves the game. If a player only steps on "stepping stones" that are off the player gets to the "Win" stepping stone. The pressure pads need to be placed on wooden boards that can be in the shape of "stepping stones" all placed on a blue background cloth indicating water that can hide the wires going to the pressure pads.

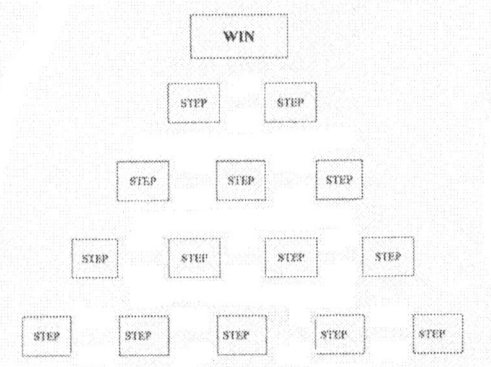

Slot Machines – and other electrical machine

The slot machines described in this section are comparatively simple compared to the complex amusement machines found in commercial arcades. These complex machines have devices incorporated into the design, which ensure that the operator will always make a profit and rely very little on the skill of the player and prevents players from shaking the machine to give a non winning pay out. The components described in this section can be incorporated into different designs and ideas for the actual games described. They can pay out automatically or ring a bell or illuminate a "win" sign, when the winning action happens, for the attendant to give out a prize.

The first slot machines were either clockwork or relied on the action of a lever to move a series of cogs, wheels, slides and engage springs like early "One Arm Bandits or Fruit Machines" where the action of pulling down the arm re-set a number of sprung coin pay out chutes and caused the dials to spin. A vast array of early mechanical machines that have been restored by enthusiasts and are often found in museums and traditional preserved fun fairs and are normally operated with heavy old coins. With today's lighter coins it is necessary to use the action of a coin against an electrical micro or proximity switch that is more sensitive than yesterday's mainly mechanical slot machines.

The basic operation for all slot machines is for the coin to operate a micro switch or to activate a proximity switch (a device which detects a metal coin passing within close range and giving a very small electrical current which will normally operate a holding circuit or switching relay). The machines described are electrically operated either from the mains supply or battery supply, with all live electrical connections protected in the correct manner with a notice on the access door or cover that the power must be isolated before opening. The cases must be sturdy and clamped or fixed in some way to a solid table to protect the machine and stop the machine being tilted to gain an unfair advantage. With all mains powered and everything using in excess of 50 volts the correct fuses or miniature circuit breakers must be incorporated into games supply. If the game or any electrical equipment is being used outside or where it may be affected by damp, steam or water, a suitably rated earth detector device must be used on the main supply connection.

These machines are for fun and not commercial exploitation, Slot Machines may be considered as gambling machines and they may not be sited in a permanent position otherwise a licence may be required. They have the advantage of not requiring an attendant and could be combined with other "penny" games making a "Penny Arcade". Although the term penny is used it can be any suitable denomination of coin provided the coin is round.

The main components of simple electrical games

Micro switch and Proximity switch

A standard micro switch is for low current and has three connections so that the switch can be used for normally closed or open when the arm is moved. A proximity switch detects the coin passing near the face of the proximity switch and requires a baffle in front to prevent the switch being operated by other metal objects. The range of the proximity switch is limited to a few mm. Proximity switches need to be used in conjunction with a switching relay to handle large currents.

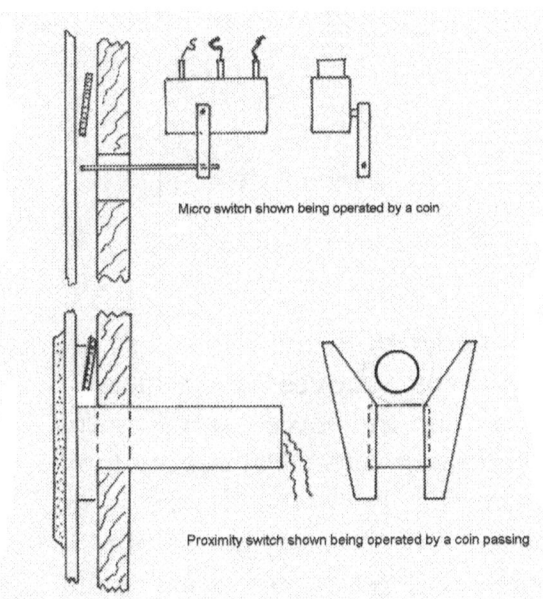

Micro switch shown being operated by a coin

Proximity switch shown being operated by a coin passing

Holding Circuit

A holding circuit switches on a device by a micro switch or proximity switch operating, momentarily closing and then opening the electrical switch. This action of the switch is sufficient to activate the holding relay moving contacts 3 and 4 to the closed position. The device 5, which may be an electric lamp, buzzer or motor, then has an electrical supply until such time as an isolating switch is opened and the relay drops out. The power supply to the device is then lost.

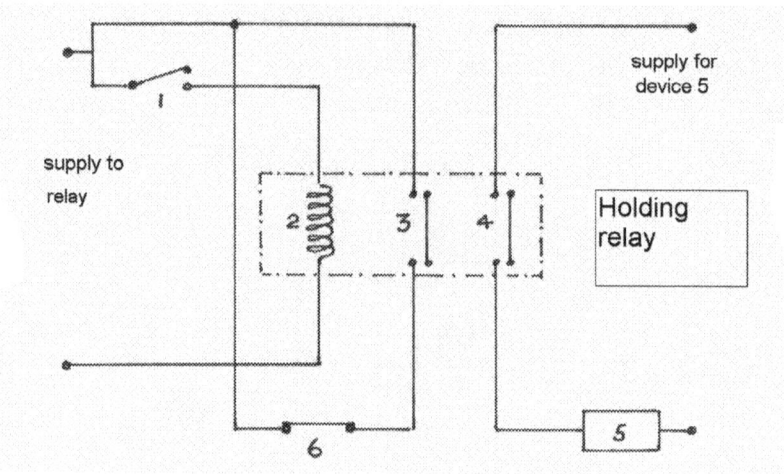

Switch 1 is operated within the game and energises the coil in the holding relay, which moves the contacts 3 to keep the circuit closed and to maintain the power supply to the coil. At the same time contacts 4 allow the electrical supply to power the device 5. When the power supply to the device is no longer required switch 6 is opened and the relay drops out. Switch 6 is then re-closed and the circuit is ready to operate again.

Jackpot Mechanism

The jackpot mechanism is a geared micro motor, which moves a little, each time a micro switch or proximity switch is operated. When the operating arm strikes the micro switch arm, a circuit is instigated through a holding circuit ringing a bell or buzzer or lighting a flashing lamp. An over-ride switch moves the micro motor around till it clears the micro switch arm and re-sets the jackpot mechanism.

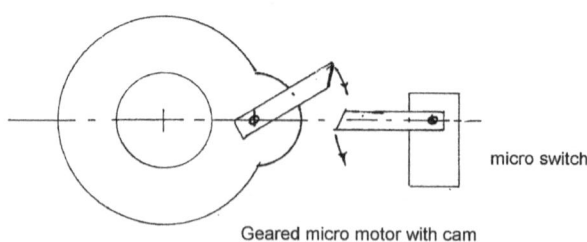

Geared micro motor with cam

Timers

Timers can be adjustable or set at a particular length of time; these are electronic devices that will require a switching relay to energise the electrical load. They can be linked to a geared micro motor with a number of contacts for switching electrical loads. Timer switches can be used either for power to the micro-motor to be on for a given time. For the purposes of automatic games the timers need to be in seconds rather than hours and minutes. You could use the jackpot mechanism as a timer depending on the speed of the micro-motor.

Pay out chute

Pay out chute can be made but need the skills of a practical engineer or they can be purchased. In simple terms the coins are stacked above a slide that is the thickness of the pay out coin. The slide is moved by the action of a magnetic coil being energised and returned, to hold the coins back, by the tension spring. Each time the slide moves it will release a coin or token into the pay out bowl. The potential winning coins are placed in the tube above the chute mechanism or can be automatically fed into the coin tube from the coins placed in the entry chute, with excess money dropping into a collection area.

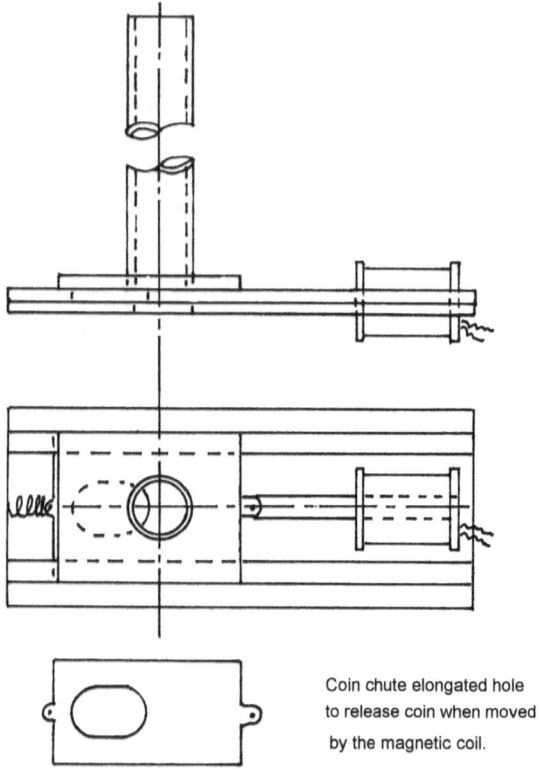

Coin chute elongated hole
to release coin when moved
by the magnetic coil.

The coin chute can pay out one or more coins by altering the thickness of the coin chute slider.

An alternative is to utilise a tray that is hinged and holds the winnings and is released by an electric magnetic coil, which could be re-cycled from a doorbell mechanism.

Coin Entry Chute

The coin entry chute ensures that coins of a smaller diameter than the play price drop through the side of the chute and returned to the player. Larger coins are prevented from entering by the coin slot. The entry slot is of a size that prevents larger diameter or thicker coins being put in.

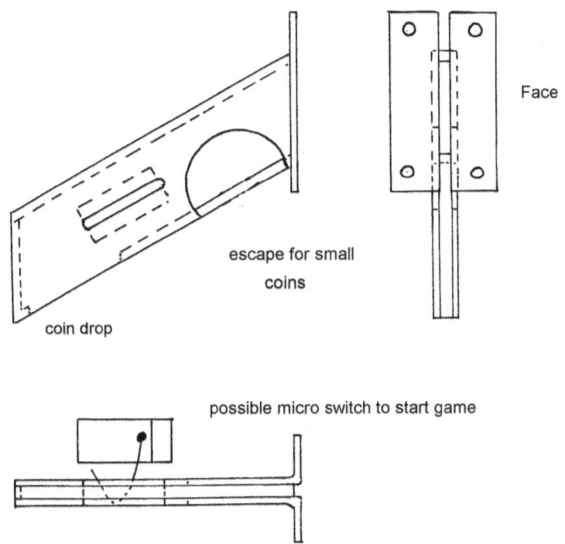

escape for small
coins

coin drop

Face

possible micro switch to start game

Slot Machines

All slot machines and other electric powered games shown need to be in wooden cabinets that for safety reasons have a locked door to the inner workings and electrical connections. The examples shown are basic ideas and the manufacture of different games depends entirely on the materials available. They all have glass / plastic fronts, which need to be supported and in the case of the Penny Falls game the top edge where the coins are dropped in must be a polished bevelled edge to prevent any cuts to fingers.

Penny Falls

This is a basic game and relies on pure luck to win. The coin denomination is variable and the use of smaller diameter valued coins can be avoided by holes above the studs that drop the smaller coins out of the game. The use of larger coins by players, can be avoided, by slots at the top that are just wide enough to take the chosen coin size.

69

The coins are placed in the top of the glass front and drop down hitting the small diameter studs, causing the coin to be deflected and either going into the win chutes or dropping into the bottom of the case as profit. If the coin goes down the win chute it operates a switch that in turn operates the pay out mechanism that gives out more than the play coin denomination.

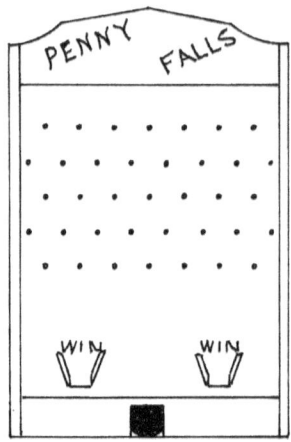

Roll a Penny

The game requires the player to move a slide bar connected to the pusher handle when the coin is over the win slot. The coin then activates a switch, which in turn operates the pay out chute

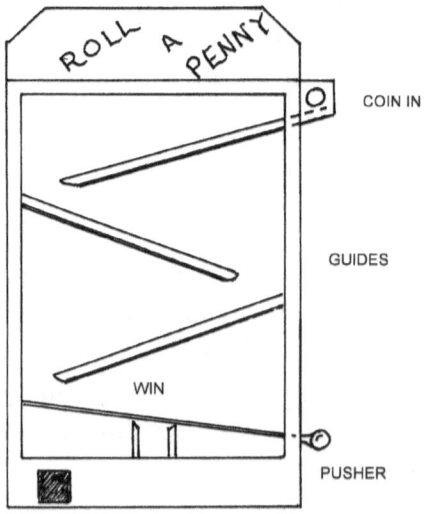

Jackpot

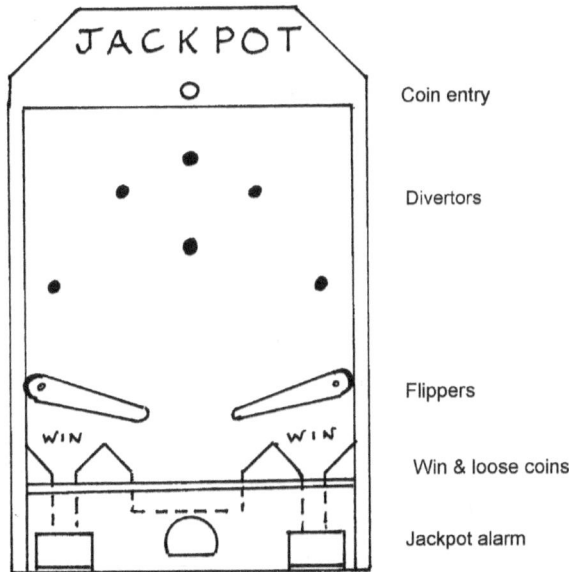

This game uses the jackpot mechanism; when the coin enters a win slot it activates a switch that in turn moves the micro motor of the jackpot mechanism. This version is shown with flippers that throw the coins around to make the game more interesting. The jackpot is indicated by an illuminated sign or ringing bell that alerts the attendant to give out the jackpot prize. The game can be constructed without any electrical components; the coins going in the "win" shoot are held on a balanced lever that releases the gathered coins when they reach a certain weight and pay out as a jackpot. There is a need to have two or three balances where the coins gathered are hidden from the player so it is a surprise win and there are other collectors waiting to pay out.

Electric Roll a Ball

This uses metal ball bearings that when entering the win chute connect an electrical circuit by two metal plates on the sides. The ball bearings need to be at least 20 mm diameter to ensure their weight will make a good connection. The making of the electrical connection will light (L) as a single lamp relating to that chute and then, when all the balls have been rolled into the different chutes lights up another lamp or bell (B), indicating a prize win for filling all the slots. To make a good electrical connection a voltage of 24 volts is needed.

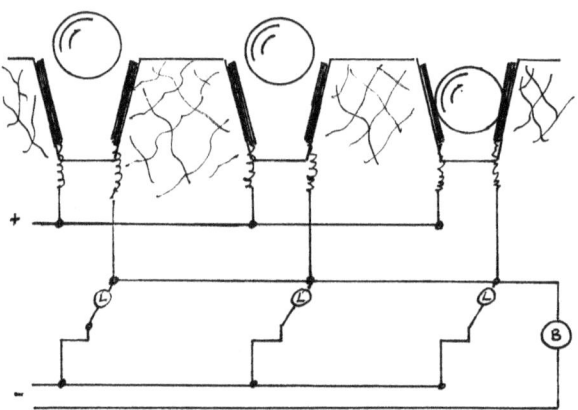

Other ideas for games

9. Prizes and goods for stalls

The obtaining of prizes and goods for sale falls into four categories:

- What is going to be donated by the supporters on a personal level?

- What can be anticipated as donations from commercial organisations?

- What has to be purchased?

- What can be manufactured cheaply?

With donations from supporters it is prudent to make up a list of items being sought that ties in with the planned stalls, otherwise you may end up with goods that cannot be sold. There are today, unfortunately, some problems with cakes and other home made edibles being offered for sale, that may not have been prepared to commercial kitchen hygiene standards. Make sure that all food offered is prepared and served in hygienic conditions including the way they are wrapped and stored or cooked and served at the recommended temperature.

Asking commercial organisations for support in providing goods from their range of products is common practice. However, many of the larger organisations have a limited budget that supports charities, which may be available. You need to ask early, possibly a year in advance, by letter to the Managing Director clearly explaining what you are organising and the good cause you are supporting with some detail on the aims of your organisation. When looking at different potential commercial supporters, consider how their product relates to your good cause, for example, it may not be prudent to seek support for a cause supporting the animal welfare if the commercial organisation tests their products on animals. Say that you will acknowledge their support in your programme or on posters displayed at the event. Always remembering to send a letter of thanks after the event telling your supporters how much you made for the cause. Most large organisations have promotional items such as pens, pencils, erasers, balloons, drinking mugs, badges, tapes or CD's, note pads, tee shirts, base ball caps, etc., all with their company logo, name or product. They are good for consolation prizes for games, if nothing else, but cannot generally be sold as such. If it's a food or drink company they may supply sample packs; these will not be for sale but instead used as consolation prizes perhaps for children who did not win in a fancy dress competition, arts & crafts competition or a sports event.

The purchase of goods for stalls and prize games needs to ensure that where possible there is a 100% mark-up on the cost of the item. Buying wholesale will provide a profit but this requires a minimum order value and agreement of the wholesaler to supply your organisation; always look for a discount if you are paying cash. Look out for closing down sales and auctions of fancy goods as a suitable source of cheap goods but remember you are buying as seen and there is little come back if the goods are not of a saleable quality. Buying goods in multiple packs and splitting them up is another way of providing low cost prizes. The biggest problem is getting prizes that can be used on games that look good and give perceived value for money, when the price of having a go, on children's games in particular, needs to be kept low.

There are companies who specialise in providing promotional goods where items can be embossed with you organisations name, event or slogan. These items include pens and pencils, erasers, rulers, booklets, boxes, hats, tee shirts, key fobs, towels. These make saleable items or prizes but there will be a minimum order for printing.

One technique is called "adding value" to a purchased item. This could be the combining of suitable items into sets and presenting the package in gift-wrapping or cellophane or cling film with a decorative ribbon. A mixture of goods that make up the components for some cooking activity with the recipe included, may be appropriate especially if linked with the theme of your event. It could even be a number of toy figures or other items in a setting that can link together with a story booklet. The perceived value of the whole is then greater than its components.

The manufacture of foodstuffs for sale or as prizes has not been included in this book mainly because it is often uneconomical and there are many recipe books on the market. Some foodstuffs that appeal mainly to children have a very high profit margin including popcorn, ice cream, prawn crackers, chips and candy floss. Many popular food items like sweets, crisps /fries and biscuits can probably be purchased in quantity at less than the price of home made sweets. Drinks like tea, coffee and squashes cost very little to make, the major fixed costs being the disposable drink containers and the drink components. Other foods for the refreshment stalls such as hot dogs, pizza and beef burgers can show a high profit margin, just as long as you can budget the amount that will be sold with some accuracy.

The following are ideas for the manufacture of prizes and goods for sale that cost little in materials. The depiction of a clown is used as it can be drawn without a great artistic ability.

Clown Pencil

This is a popular gift made with a white table tennis ball (use the cheap toy shop versions rather than the professional sports balls), for the head. With care the table tennis ball is drilled to take a standard pencil. The "head" is then filled with a few grains of rice, to make it rattle, and the top of the pencil glued into the ball. The head is then fitted with a conical shaped hat made from felt and glued to the "head", you could also introduce some strands of wool to make a resemblance of comical hair. The head is then painted with a nose and mouth and using "wobbly" eyes from craft supplies. The final touch is a little scarf between the top of the pencil and the "head". To increase the sales potential it is a good idea to make a base stand from either a scrap of timber with holes to take the pencil tips or a block of polystyrene will suffice. This will give a good display and also prevent the pencils from being damaged.

Flower Box

The flower box is a block of timber, about 200 mm square and 400 mm long, drilled with a number of holes and painted a dark colour. The holes will take plastic flowers. The sides of the block of timber are slatted with sections of wood about 10 mm by 3 mm, these slats are pre-varnished with clear varnish and glued on as shown in the picture. Finally the artificial flowers are "planted" in the holes and the item is ready for sale.

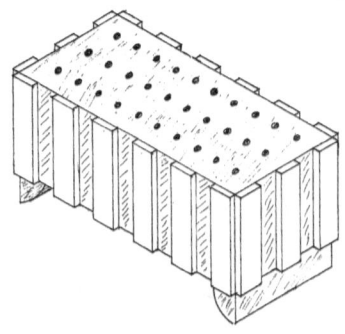

Pom-Poms

These are a cheap gift to make from odd lengths of knitting wool. They are made by cutting out two card discs, 150mm diameter with a centre hole 15mm diameter. These cards are placed together and wool is wound around and through the centre of the disc using a large needle. When no more wool can be threaded through the centre hole the wool is cut between the two cards discs using a craft knife. The "string" that holds the strands of wool together and holds the pom-pom, is provided, by using either a length of ribbon or elastic, a knot is tied between the two card discs to secure the woollen threads. The card discs are then cut out and the pom-pom is ready with perhaps a little tidying up of long ends. A mixture of bright coloured wools can be used or pinks, whites or blues for babies.

Bookmarks

This is a cheap to make prize or sale item using a piece of thin card with a length of ribbon attached to the card. The card needs to be about 40 mm wide and 200 mm long with a piece of ribbon some 100 mm long. The actual card can be produced on the computer with some suitable ClipArt or a short verse to suit the event. For added value the paper can be laminated to make them durable and enhance the appearance. Children's versions can be produced in the shape of a cartoon character a simple clown or sitting cat shape. This item could be linked to the sale of a book to give added value.

Badges

Badges can be made using a commercially available badge-making machine with the blanks and plastic front covers, you produce the artwork that is sandwiched between the base and the plastic cover and pressed together.

A cheaper way is to purchase "conference delegate" badges that are made from card or plastic. These are already fitted with a fixing pin or clip. These badges are then covered with a suitable design or perhaps a cartoon character printed from the computer on card and glued to the base badge. With a Christmas or Easter theme a purchased decoration could be fixed to the badge.

The artwork for the face of the badge could be personalised, if you have a supporter who is skilled in calligraphy or an artist, with the name of the person buying the badge.

An added feature could be to fix a short compression spring to the base badge with a character shape fixed on its back to the spring giving a wobbling badge.

Circus Jugglers

This toy is constructed from a cardboard tube about 120 mm diameter and 75 mm long. A card base is glued to the tube and a cellophane top made that will be fixed to the top of the tube. The inside of the tube has a paper covering that depicts a circus audience and the outside of the tube is decorated to look like a circus tent. Small clown figures (spread eagled) are cut out from coloured tissue paper and put inside the "circus". The cellophane lid is then fixed in place. By gently rubbing the cellophane with the fingers, static electricity is generated and the clown figures start to jump about. Suitable cellophane can be re-cycled from display boxes for packs of Christmas cards, boxes of nuts etc.

Trinket Boxes

Small boxes can be easily made from sheet timber. The trick is to make the box as hollow shape marking where the top and bottom sections will divide, then fix the hinges in place. After the hinges are fitted and removed, the box shape is sawn into the two halves and the hinges re-fitted. The fitting of a musical box movement is possible, however, the cost of the movement may be uneconomical considering the likely sale price of the item.

Boxes can also be made of card or purchased from a card shop. The boxes can be decorated to suit the theme of the event. Mystery contents boxes on the jewellery stall may be appropriate.

Pop-up Clown

The pop-up clown is made from a wooden ball that is painted as a clowns face. The wooden ball has a hole drilled that takes the operating stick. The clown's top is made of bright cloth material and its base is a cardboard cone. This is a child's gift that is easy to make once you get the pattern right so it is best to make one first then copy the pattern of shapes to cut from card or material.

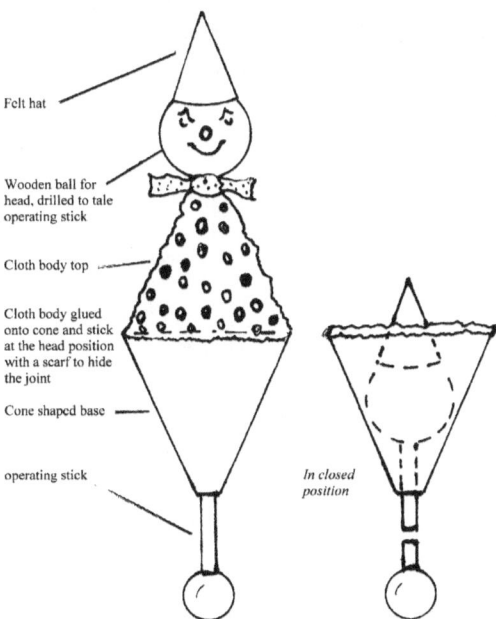

Matchbox Stand

This consists of a small base that has a rectangular-shaped piece of wood glued to it, providing a stand for a slightly open standard matchbox. The rectangular piece of wood is sized to slide into the outer cover of a matchbox and 10 mm high. The small base can be of polished or varnished wood, plastic sheet, thick card or some other material. The base is decorated with a shell, polished pebble, a Christmas cake decoration, an Easter chick or anything else, which ties in with the actual event.

Flower Basket

This can be a display of fresh or artificial flowers in a suitable container that is not too large and eye catching. The planting of bulbs in a container so that they are nearly ready for the event is a reasonable moneymaker and suitable for Spring and Christmas events with hyacinths for the latter. Another option is to use supple thin twigs that are made into a basket that is packed with moss and compost then planted with polyanthus / primrose or a similar plant.

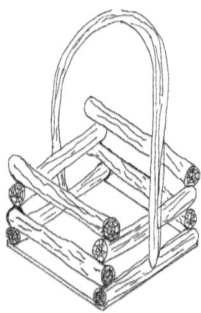

Mirror Flowers

By obtaining from a supplier a framed mirror no larger than A4 size the mirror is enhanced with a simple decoration that will increase the saleability and provide an unusual gift. A small clear or coloured plastic or wooden box (just the sides, front and base) is made and "super-glued" to the mirror in its bottom right or left hand corner. The box is then filled with dried flowers that will be reflected in the mirror, which can be hung from a wall or left as a freestanding mirror.

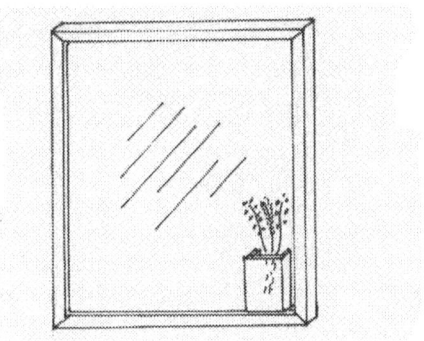

Bird Puppet

The bird puppet is a simple string puppet that is made with thick card or thin wood with the feet and wings connected to the body with coloured cord. The eyes are the plastic wobbly eyes from craft suppliers and the tail is a feather.

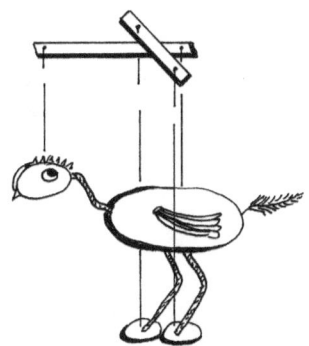

Finger Puppet

Finger puppets are made of felt with suitable hats and faces. They can also be made utilising a pair of small size woollen gloves, and embroidering different faces on the fingertips.

Another version is to design a face and body with two finger holes (for the fingers to go through making the legs). The shape is then printed on card with the "leg" holes suitable for a child's fingers and then cut out. These can be comical characters where the child puts the fingers through the holes and makes the puppet walk or dance.

Glove Puppets

Glove puppets need a cloth body that has three fingers, one for the head and two for the arms, with plenty of room for the two folded fingers. The head can be moulded from moulding plastic and then covered with paper mache this is simply small pieces of tissue paper soaked in water-based paste and moulded over the plastic shape. Once the paper mache is dried and hard the plastic material is removed from the inside of the head and the head painted then fixed to the body. The head shape could also be made from a rubber / plastic ball with a hole drilled to take the finger that moves the head.

An alternative is a puppet on a stick with thin wires attached to the "hands" to move the arms about. In this case the head can be a wooden or polystyrene ball supported on a stick that also holds the body in place.

Marionettes

Marionettes or string puppets can be simple or complicated. The ideas described are for simple puppets that can be made easily. The head of the doll is made using a painted wooden ball or dolls face onto a base with the torso made as two blocks of wood and the arms and legs made of small diameter doweling. The body components being wood are connected together using hook screw eyes. The body is then dressed in cloth material. Strings are attached to the head, shoulder, hands, legs and feet. The strings are attached to the operating cross making sure that the length of the various strings balances the body and keeps the head upright. When packaging the finished puppet making sure that the strings do not become tangled, by wrapping in cling film.

Penny Plain Tuppence Coloured Theatre

This is a traditional puppet theatre where the puppets are card figures fixed to a slat of wood or thin card that moves the characters around the stage. The name originating because in days past, the printed sheets in colour were dearer if they were printed in just black outline for the constructor to colour in and build their own toy theatre. The theatre can be any size and linked to a particular story where you can provide a typed up script that links with the characters and scenes. The item needs a solid base with the front of the theatre stage, the proscenium, cut out and pasted to a hardboard backing with side wings and back cloths pasted onto hardboard backings that slot into the stage base. The theatre can be as complex or simple as you like with curtains, lights, changing scenes and even a musical box movement incorporated. This item needs to be boxed and can represent a modern or traditional theatre.

Booklets

The booklet is produced on A4 size paper, in landscape orientation, that will be printed / photocopied on both sides then folded to make an A5 size booklet. The pages are then stapled or stitched at the fold to form the booklet. When producing the text / pictures on a computer or by pasting onto A4 paper the same indentation needs to be maintained for the pages, if this was an 18 page booklet the layout would be as follows.

Cover – The cover needs to be a thin card or thick paper that is coloured. With the A4 paper in landscape the indentation from the left and right side of the paper should be 15mm with an indentation of 15mm either side of the centre line of the paper when folded. The left hand side will be the back cover with the name of the organisation; the right hand side will be the front cover with the title of the booklet. When folded this will make the front and back cover of the booklet.

Pages – The pages will be normal photocopy or computer print paper of a thickness that allows printing on both sides. The indentation from the right and left sides of the paper should be 10mm with an indentation of 15mm either side of the centre line of the paper when folded. With page 1 on the left side, page 18 will be on the right side then as follows: - left page 17 right page 2, left page 3 right page 16, left page 15 right page 4, left page 5 right page 14, left page 13 right page 6, left page 7 right page 12, left page 11 right page 8 and left page 9 right page 10.

The topics for the booklet could be a collection of recipes, poems, short stories, local history, personal recollections, local guidebook, gardening hints, jokes and funny stories, perhaps with a lucky number printed inside linked to a prize, etc. The booklet could also be a Children's Puzzle Book, with quizzes, word games, dot-to-dot pictures, outlines to colour in, simple crosswords, jokes, and competition to enter suiting all to suit the age group of the target readership. This could be a Christmas Booklet given out by a Father Christmas in his grotto, to include a letter for children to complete and send to "Santa Claus" saying what they would like for Christmas.

The booklets are reasonably cheap to produce and can be sold for three times the cost of the computer printing or photocopying, depending on the quality of the booklet produced. As the real cost is the printing, the higher the number printed / photocopied, the lower the production cost. However, it may be possible to produce a number of different booklets on various subjects, as the printing cost is predictable. They can also be used for prizes that are unique to your event and perhaps sold afterwards if they are left depending on the circumstances.

Books

Booklets that have lined or blank pages can be purchased and then converted into special usage books. A new front page is produced, either on the computer or photocopied artwork. This new cover is pasted onto the cover using spray glue that will dry without marking the new cover. The books could be: "Telephone Numbers", "Secrets", "Gardening Records", "Telephone Messages", "Memory Jogger", "Sketch Book", "Recipes", "Contacts", "Autographs", "My Little Black Book", "E-mail Addresses", "Joke Book", "My Stories", etc. The original books are available cheaply and the conversions will double the purchased value. They can be used as sale items or game prizes that are special to your event.

Periscope

The periscope is made of card with a mirror at each end so that you can view over the heads of others. The card tube is about 600 mm long and 100 by 150 mm covered with suitable stickers or painted. It is possible to use a plastic sheet with a mirror finish instead of glass mirrors to remove any risk of the glass breaking.

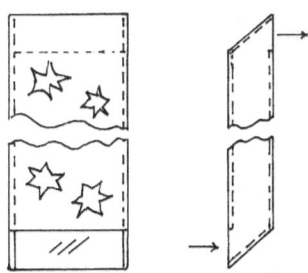

Lavender Bag

Lavender bags are made from a suitably printed cotton cloth sewn into a small open top bag that is tied with ribbon at the top. The bag needs to be about 40 mm square, with the top either hemmed or cut with pinking scissors. The bag is filled with dried lavender that can either be purchased or collected in the autumn from garden plants and dried out in a paper bag. You could also use "pot-puree" (scented dried flowers), which is readily available, to fill the bag. Make sure that the finished product is kept in a sealed container, to prevent the aroma from fading, till the event. It is also possible to make **Christmas Tree Decorations** with the bags made of green and red material and the bags filled with suitable spices that give off a "yuletide" aroma.

Balloon on a Stick

Normal balloons are inflated and tied to a wooden or plastic stick. The item could be made a little different by sticking self-adhesive coloured paper or plastic shapes and possibly incorporating a painted as a clown's face onto the inflated balloon. The balloon can also be filled with rice, small balls or cereals to make a noise or even a small soft toy) to give added interest, (making sure the contents are not a danger to young children). It is possible to purchase special sticks that have a loop at the top that holds the inflated balloon in place.

Plaster Figures

Using purchased rubber moulds of figures, animals and other shapes for plaster casting from craft suppliers. The use of dental plaster or fine grade plaster is much cheaper than the plaster sold by craft shops. The plaster cast must be left to dry fully which could take 28 days depending on the weather and storage conditions. The base of the figure once fully dried can be filed flat with a rasp or by rubbing onto course sandpaper that is on a flat surface. By choosing a plaster cast that is easy to paint in just one main colour, with the minimum of other decoration, will ensure a professional end product. The figures can be painted with a water-based paint and varnished. The base should be covered with felt or card that has a "felt" surface finish that is slightly larger than the base of the model. **Hint**, make sure that when the plaster is poured into the mould, the mould is flexed to ensure there are no air bubbles trapped, which may cause holes in the finished cast; some holes could be filled with plaster afterwards if the air hole is easy to fill making sure the repair has time to dry before painting.

Larger rubber moulds can be purchased for making garden gnomes and other ornaments for the garden and cast in fine concrete. They can be painted, however, they need to fully dry out this will take longer than the plaster casts.

Hot Plate

Hot plates can be made cheaply by purchasing sample ceramic floor tiles that are covered on the back by self-adhesive plastic floor tiles. Alternatively a wooden picture frame can be made with a wooden (hardboard or plywood) backing sheet, to take the tile. The wood needs to be varnished or sealed to prevent water damage. Smaller versions for teapot stands can be made using ceramic wall tiles.

Calendars

Some computer programs for processing digital photographs have the facility to print calendars attached to a photograph. This can provide a very professional gift especially if the photographs are of local scenes.

Another alternative is to purchase calendars in book form and attach to a suitable picture to hang on a wall.

Purchase cheap pocket diaries and cover them with a new cover, that relates to your good cause, a local interest or a mixture of new covers to suit different age groups. If the facilities are available with a computer and printer you could devise a layout for the cover that you can type in the name of the diaries owner, which is then printed and spray glued to the diary at your event.

Christmas Log

The Christmas Log is made from dried out cut branches from any tree. The log should be about 45 mm diameter and 200 mm long. The ends should be filed and sanded flat and one side of the length of the log planned flat. Two holes are drilled in the top (opposite side to the planned surface) to take medium sizes candles. The log is then varnished with clear varnish and allowed to dry fully. The completed log is then made into a table centre by placing the candles in the holes and fixing Christmas cake decoration together with a good wishes message. The finished logs can be sold or used as tombola or raffle prizes at a pre-Christmas event.

Table Candle

The table candle needs a base that could be a small plate or saucer or a wooden shape. Use a small length of plastic or metal tubing that has an inside diameter a little larger than the diameter of the chosen candle. The tubing is "super glued" to the base. With the tubing in place make an infill on the base with plaster that has had some powder paint added to the mix, while the plaster is wet fix some pebbles, shells, nuts, Christmas decorations, plastic flowers etc., onto the plaster. Once everything is dry the base can be varnished and the candle put in place, ready for sale.

Cube Dispenser

This is a wall mounted dispenser for "OXO" cubes or similar and is made from timber mouldings glued together, sanded and varnished or polished. The item is presented for sale with the cubes in place.

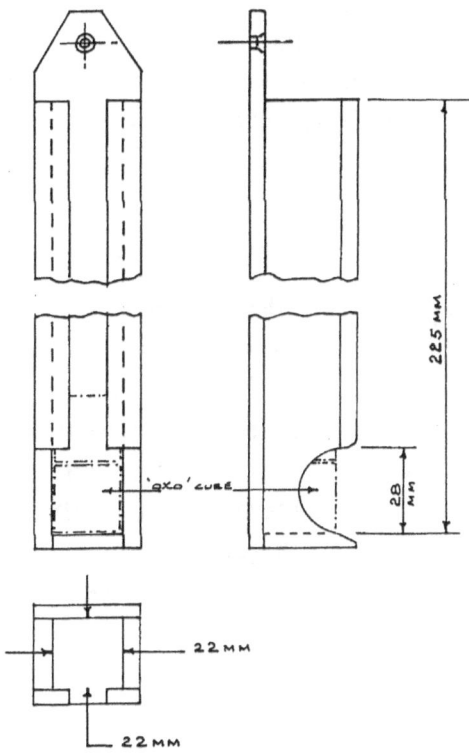

Gift Poetry

By using a computer program an A4 sheet is produced with a boarder and a suitable poem (that is out of copyright) typed in a fancy font. Colour print using a heavy weight coloured paper. The sheet is then rolled and tied with a coloured ribbon as a presentation gift. This is a low cost item to produce and could be linked with other items such as a fancy handkerchief, towel or toiletries to make a more expensive looking prize or stall product.

Mobiles

Mobiles can be made using painted shapes cut from plywood and strung to a frame with plastic wire. The shapes can be of any design but they need to be painted on both sides. The mobile can incorporate chimes or operated from a musical box movement.

Whirligig

This is a very cheap prize to make and consists of a piece of coloured card about 80mm diameter. The card has painted shapes, stickers or a spiral on both sides. The card has two holes punched at a radius of 5 mm from the centre and opposite each other. A loop of cord (total length 1m) goes through the holes. The toy is used by flexing the loop of cord with each hand moving inwards and outwards, getting the whirligig whirling around and making a noise. This could make a nice low value gift as a consolation prize or even a lucky dip prize.

Boxes of Sweets / Candy

Simply an added value gift using a standard gift box that has some added decoration then filled with sweets, nuts, chocolates, biscuits etc. It could also be a china mug, cup and saucer, or some other container all wrapped in cellophane and tied with a ribbon.

Tee Shirts

Computer programs are available to produce stencils on a special paper that is then ironed onto a plain tee shirt, and the motif transferred permanently onto the cloth. This could be a design linked to the event or to advertise your own good cause. It could be used as a uniform for all the helpers as well as a highly saleable item. It can also be used for handkerchiefs, towels and other cloth items. There are commercial companies that undertake the supply of specially printed tee shirts, towels etc. You can also have items machine embroidered by specialist companies onto cloth items but this is a more expensive option.

An alternative is to look out for material, "off the roll" that has suitable motives that can be cut out and sown to the tee shirt or heat glued.

More prize ideas

10 After the event

There are a number of important things to do after the event to ensure that your next event will be even more successful.

- Thank you letters to major contributors, telling them how well you have done and looking forward to their support in the future.

- Newspaper article telling the readers how the good cause will benefit together with a selection of photographs of the activities that the Editor may like to use.

- Lessons learnt discussion with the organising committee is always worthwhile and keeps a record of what really occurred.

- Publish the total profit from the event once all the income and expenditure is known.

- Did the effort reflect the profit made?

- Did the event increase the awareness of the organisation and its objectives in a positive manner?

- Did the organiser have an enjoyable experience and feel the whole experience was satisfying?

- Make sure any re-usable items, games etc., are stored safely away for the next time.

- Start to plan the next event.

Personal Thoughts

Did you enjoy the Money Making experience?

Was everyone happy?

Did you cope with the weather?

Were your personal needs catered for?

Would you do it again?

www.ingramcontent.com/pod-product-compliance
Lightning Source LLC
Chambersburg PA
CBHW022115170526
45157CB00004B/1657